ALEXIS DE TOCQUEVILLE

Eminent Lives—brief biographies by distinguished authors on canonical figures—joins a long tradition in this lively form, from Plutarch's *Lives* to Vasari's *Lives of the Painters*, Dr. Johnson's *Lives of the Poets* to Lytton Strachey's *Eminent Victorians*. Pairing great subjects with writers known for their strong sensibilities and sharp, lively points of view, the Eminent Lives are ideal introductions designed to appeal to the general reader, the student, and the scholar. "To preserve a becoming brevity which excludes everything that is redundant and nothing that is significant," wrote Strachey: "That, surely, is the first duty of the biographer."

ALSO BY JOSEPH EPSTEIN

Friendship: An Exposé

Snobbery: The American Version

Fabulous Small Jews

Envy: The Seven Deadly Sins

Narcissus Leaves the Pool: Familiar Essays

A Line Out for a Walk: Familiar Essays

Partial Payments: Essays on Writers and Their Lives

Life Sentences: Literary Essays

With My Trousers Rolled: Familiar Essays

Ambition: The Secret Passion

Once More Around the Block: Familiar Essays

Goldin Boys: Stories

Plausible Prejudices: Essays on American Writing

ALEXIS DE TOCQUEVILLE

Democracy's Guide

Joseph Epstein

EMINENT LIVES

ATLAS BOOKS

HarperCollins*Publishers*

ALEXIS DE TOCQUEVILLE. Copyright © 2006 by Joseph Epstein. All
rights reserved. Printed in the United States of America. No part of
this book may be used or reproduced in any manner whatsoever without written permission except in the case of brief quotations embodied
in critical articles and reviews. For information, address HarperCollins
Publishers, 10 East 53rd Street, New York, NY 10022.

HarperCollins books may be purchased for educational, business, or
sales promotional use. For information, please write: Special Markets
Department, HarperCollins Publishers, 10 East 53rd Street, New York,
NY 10022.

FIRST EDITION

Designed by Elliott Beard

Library of Congress Cataloging-in-Publication Data is available upon
request.

ISBN-10: 0-06-059898-0
ISBN-13: 978-0-06-059898-3

06 07 08 09 10   ID/RRD   10 9 8 7 6 5 4 3 2 1

For Maurice Rosenfield
(1914–2005)

Intelligence is the power of seeing things
in the past, present, and future as
they have been, are, and will be.

—GEORGE SANTAYANA
Letter to Horace Meyer Kallen, March 15, 1917

Alexis de Tocqueville

Introduction

WHAT WOULD Count Alexis de Tocqueville (1805–1859), were he alive today, have made of *le phénomène de Tocqueville*? *Le phénomène* is of course not merely Tocqueville's continuing but his increasing fame. Today if one reads about America, about democracy, about liberty, about bureaucracy, about equality, about almost any aspect of politics, or for that matter about large stretches of human nature as it emerges in a political context, one sooner or later encounters Tocqueville. To anyone writing about these subjects he all too often seems to have made one's point long ago and usually much better than one could have done on one's own. One might think to paraphrase him, even plagiarize him, but in the end it makes much more sense merely to quote him and move along.

And people have been quoting Tocqueville, relentlessly, for nearly two centuries. Nowadays he pops up in earnest letters to the *New York Times:* "It behooves us, however, to remember that Tocqueville warns … " He is brought in to defend or argue against all sorts of arrangements in which he himself is likely to have had less than passionate interest; in college sports, for example, "Tocqueville and College Football" was the title of an article in the December 29, 2003, issue of the *Weekly Standard*. Sociologists, political scientists, and American presidents are fond of quoting him on behalf of their own arguments and positions: "Tocqueville might also have agreed with my claim," the sociologist Herbert Gans recently wrote, "that in a corporate-dominated America, the journalists' approach to informing citizens can do little to keep our democracy representative." Benedict XVI, early in his papacy, has already cited Tocqueville. For all one knows, God himself may have quoted Tocqueville.

Tocqueville is one of that select circle of writers more often quoted than read. There is even a false Tocqueville quotation going the rounds—"America is great because America is good, and if America ceases to be good, she will cease to be great"— that has been used by Senator John Kerry, former president Bill Clinton, and who knows how many Republican politicians.

Suggesting the beginnings of a backlash, in the June 5, 2005, issue of the *New York Times Book Review*, a reviewer writes: "A good rule of thumb for assessing sociopolitical books is: The more often the name 'Tocqueville' appears, the more numbing and uninsightful the work will be." Let us hope this is not true, for if it is, the book in your hands is clearly a dead item.

When the first part of Tocqueville's *Democracy in America* was published in 1835, it was an immediate success, first in France and then in English translation. Because it viewed America so favorably, it was often used in the United States as a school text. The second part, published in 1840—which was much more critical, expanded the subject greatly to include the complications brought on by the spread of equality, and had much wider application than to America alone—did not do so well, either critically or commercially. After his death, Tocqueville's book seemed to share the fate of most books: to fall gradually into oblivion, though it managed to remain in print. But in 1938, a Tocqueville revival began, owing partly to the discovery of a large collection of Tocqueville's manuscripts and papers, including diaries, travel notes, and letters written home to France from America. Suddenly, too, the second part of *Democracy in America*, with its subtle critique of the spirit of equality, its animadversions on bureaucracy, and its concern with the element of mediocrity inherent in democracy, began to seem much more pertinent in its application to modern societies. Taken up and elucidated by such thinkers as Raymond Aron in France, Tocqueville's writings attracted more interest, and his reputation was revived—a revival that shows no sign of flagging.

Tocqueville's fame is owed to his powers of analysis and trenchancy of formulation. A woman remarked on meeting Henry James for the first time that she had never seen a man "so assailed by the perceptions." Tocqueville, in like manner, was assailed by the desire—though the word "need" is perhaps more accurate—to analyze all social arrangements and political institutions that passed before him. He did so with a very high degree of accurate perception. But it is not enough to perceive accurately. The full art of observation entails not only seeing but composing what one has seen with concision and force in a form that is both striking and memorable. "In politics," Tocqueville wrote, "shared hatreds are almost always the basis of friendships." He also wrote: "History is a gallery of pictures in which there are few originals and many copies." And—can this be improved on as an explanation of why so many intellectuals have been so foolish in their political views?—"How a great mind, joined to a weak soul, sometimes serves to increase the weakness of the latter! The brilliant faculties of the one give reason and color to the cowardice of the other." As they say in gymnastics, he nails it, time and time and yet time again.

Tocqueville is of course also famous for a number of statements that turned out to be prophetic, though it has been claimed that he is given too much credit in his role as prophet. Some of his prophecies are disputed; others amaze by their long-range accuracy. In the latter category is his by now well-known remark, at the end of the first part of *Democracy in America,* about the United States and Russia being the two nations likely to struggle for hegemony in the century ahead.

There are, at the present time, two great nations in the world which seem to tend towards the same end, although they started from different points: I allude to the Russians and the Americans.... All other nations seem to have nearly reached their natural limits, and only to be charged with the maintenance of their power;

but these are still in the act of growth; all others are stopped, or continue to advance with extreme difficulty; these are proceeding with ease and with celerity along a path to which the human eye can assign no term.... Their starting point is different, and their courses are not the same; yet each of them seems to be marked out by the will of Heaven to sway the destinies of half the globe.

Nailed it again.

Tocqueville's reputation has remained so great owing in part to the interesting fact that, after all these years, no one has quite been able to nail him—nor even to nail him down—into a clear category of thinker. Was he a political scientist, a sociologist, a philosophical historian, an intellectual interested chiefly in the play of ideas, or a politician (a failed one, finally, as we shall see) with literary gifts? Was he a genius of disinterested objectivity, or a soured aristocrat barely able to disguise his disappointment with the direction of worldly events in the elegance of his prose? He has been considered each and all of these things by the various writers who have studied and written about him since his early success, at the age of thirty, with the publication of the first volume of *Democracy in America*.

Nor is there anything resembling a consensus about Tocqueville's own politics. Political factions claim Tocqueville—as they claim George Orwell, a lesser figure—for their camps: he thus becomes a liberal for liberals, a conservative for conservatives, a libertarian for libertarians, and so on. "An interesting list could be compiled," John Lukacs writes, "with the names of those who have asserted that Tocqueville was a conservative, a liberal, a historian, a sociologist, an aristocrat, a bourgeois, a Christian, an agnostic, for in quite a number of instances the commentators contradict themselves, and at times Tocqueville is assigned to contradictory categories in the same book, essay, or review."

Most of the time, though, Tocqueville turns out to be something rather close to the writer describing him, or at least what that writer takes himself to be. This is analogous to the time when men used to write books about Jesus Christ and discover, lo, if one were an advertising man that Jesus was the first great advertising man (Bruce Barton wrote such a book), or if one were a journalist that Jesus was the first great journalist (Lord Beaverbrook wrote such a book). John Lukacs, for example, calls Tocqueville "a great Christian thinker with a noble heart." For me he has a mind of exquisite subtlety, drenched in a Jewish-like dubiety and anxiety, with a lovely literary sensibility.

A vast amount has been written about Alexis de Tocqueville, including three full-dress biographies published in English. (The most recent, by Hugh Brogan, is due to be published in 2006.) Almost every facet of his life and thought has been taken up at length by scholars in the social sciences. What does this leave the author of this book, who is neither a scholar nor a social scientist? I wasn't sure myself until I came across a sentence that Tocqueville wrote about a book he planned but did not live long enough to write on Napoleon. The sentence reads: "Everything which shows his thoughts, his passions, finally his true self, should attract my attention." My own ambition in respect to Tocqueville, nowhere so great, is to attempt to understand what drove him to become the extraordinary writer that he was. What in his past caused him to come at his subjects as he did? What I hope to be able to do in this book is to get at the quality of the extraordinary mind that wrote *Democracy in America* and other works. In doing so I hope to understand better why Alexis de Tocqueville is one of the most engaging figures in intellectual history, and what makes him so attractive a thinker in our own time.

Chapter One

ALEXIS-CHARLES-HENRI Clérel de Tocqueville was born in Paris on July 29, 1805, but his entering the world at all was a near thing. Not that there were complications at his birth, but twelve years earlier, the Reign of Terror, as the systematically violent aftermath of the French Revolution is known, came perilously close to doing away with his parents.

Hervé de Tocqueville, Alexis's father, had married one of the granddaughters of Chrétien-Guillaume de Lamoignon de Malesherbes. A lawyer, Malesherbes had unsuccessfully defended King Louis XVI against the charge of treason before the Convention, the tribunal formed by the revolutionary French government for trying enemies of the new state. Before the revolution, he was known primarily as a man of letters who, under the reign of Louis XV, had given official permission for the publication of the great French *Encyclopédie*. He was also a correspondent and protector of Jean-Jacques Rousseau. But during the Terror, Malesherbes was sent to the guillotine as were his sister, his daughter, his son-in-law, and another granddaughter and her husband.

The twenty-one-year-old Hervé de Tocqueville and his wife Louise were rounded up along with other family members on the night of December 17, 1793, at the country estate of Malesherbes, and imprisoned in Paris. Hervé and Louise de Tocqueville watched as uncles, aunts, and cousins went off to "the Barber," as the guillotine was called, and themselves escaped owing to the luck of docket scheduling and the timely (for them) fall from power of Robespierre, who was himself guillotined on July 28, 1794.

One effect of this frightening episode, as every biographer of Tocqueveille has noted, was to turn Hervé de Tocqueville's hair white in his twenties. After the Terror was ended, he used to nap every day between three and four in the afternoon, thereby blocking out three-thirty P.M., the exact time that aristocrats were called before the revolutionary tribunal to receive their death sentences. His wife's nerves were shattered by her prison experience, and, struggle though she did to recover her health, she never quite succeeded in regaining full emotional equilibrium. As André Jardin, Tocqueville's excellent biographer, writes: "In the various accounts of [Louise de Tocqueville] that we possess, we see her as capricious, impatient, apparently also wasteful, a victim of recurring migraine headaches, and afflicted with a profound, constant melancholy that must have been quite common among the survivors of the Reign of Terror." Yet even in this saddened condition, she attempted to keep up her end of family life and was said to be helpful to the poor. Alexis de Tocqueville inherited his mother's often melancholy spirit, fits of anxiety, and fragile health.

The revolution darkened Alexis's youth and that of his older brothers, Hippolyte and Édouard, and haunted all his mature years. Why the revolution had happened, what it wrought, and which precisely were its continuing effects on French life— these were to be among the main concerns behind all Tocqueville's writing.

The Tocqueville lands and family history were long anchored in Normandy. Like so many aristocrats before the revolution, Hervé de Tocqueville favored strong reform of the laws while retaining a respectful loyalty to the Bourbon monarchy; he was among the party known as Legitimist, and he served the monarchy, at considerable personal expense, during the Bourbon restoration between 1814 and 1830. But in the eye of the furious storm that was the Terror, sympathy with reform was obliterated by the fact of aristocratic birth. When one examines the roll call of those who met their end by the blade, one discovers that the road beneath the tumbril in which aristocrats were driven to the guillotine was paved with generous liberal sentiments.

Alexis de Tocqueville, in his many reflections on the ancien régime (the time before the French Revolution), made special note of the aristocrats who gave up all the once traditional leadership responsibilities of their class, keeping and enjoying only the privileges and finally the empty pretensions of aristocratic standing. His own family was not of this kind. His father took a professional interest and an active part in local government. His cousin on his wife's side was the writer and diplomat François-René de Chateaubriand, author of *Mémoires d'outre-tombe* and other works. Chateaubriand preceded Alexis in visiting America; under the Empire he served Napoleon (whom he would later brilliantly and relentlessly attack) as a diplomat representing French interests in Rome; later, he served Louis XVIII and Charles X under the restoration. Chateaubriand claimed that aristocracies went through three phases: that of duty, that of privilege, and that of vanity. Alexis de Tocqueville, like his father, never deserted the phase of duty, in his lifetime serving on government commissions, in the various legislative assemblies, and briefly as foreign minister under Louis-Napoléon.

As a youngest and somewhat sickly son, Alexis grew up in a cocoon of affection. (People said that, even in later life, there was always something of the spoiled child about him.) He loved his father without complication, even though they often differed in their political views and in their methods of writing history. Hervé de Tocqueville was the author of *A Philosophical History of the Reign of Louis XV* and of a *Survey of the Reign of Louis XV* as well as of a volume of memoirs. In the Beinecke Rare Book and Manuscript Library at Yale, there is a painting of the handsome Hervé de Tocqueville, hair brushed forward in the style of the day, wearing the medal of the Legion of Honor, standing before his desk, with his young son Alexis behind him, seated at the desk, presumably taking his father's dictation. Count Hervé de Tocqueville died at eighty-four, preceding his son in death by only three years.

Talk about books and ideas was part of the Tocqueville family atmosphere. Precision in the use of language was also inculcated early, and, in Alexis's case, never abandoned; always a careful critic of language and its uses, he would later be a great scourge of empty phrases and self-servingly deceptive political terms.

During the Bourbon restoration, Hervé de Tocqueville served as prefect, or chief administrative official, in, among other places, Dijon, Metz, Amiens, and Versailles. When he grew older, Alexis joined his father at some of these posts, learning a good deal at first hand about the practical details of everyday politics. An appreciation for the intricate details of government is one thing that sets Tocqueville above so many other historians of government then and now, historians whose want of practical knowledge often reduces them to mere theoreticians.

Alexis was precocious, the sort of boy who reads and comprehends books supposedly well beyond his age. At school he won many of the prizes that have always been at the heart of the French lycée system. More than precocious, more than simply a good student, he was thoughtful from an early age. Sainte-Beuve, the great French literary critic, remarked that Tocqueville was of the cast of mind that "thought before it learned." In later life, his extraordinary powers of perception and stamina for concentrated meditation allowed him to contemplate what he had seen and read until he was able to tease out persuasive answers to the questions presented by his observations.

Some of Alexis's early depth as a thinker derived from his

instruction by the abbé Lesueur, his teacher, who had earlier been his father's tutor. Despite his delicacy with his young charge, the abbé drove home the lesson of original sin, imbuing Alexis with a strong sense that right action required moral character. Moral character, as Alexis would later conclude when he contemplated the connections between political and civil society, was required if men were to have any hope of exercising freedom in an enlightened and honorable way. Abbé Lesueur himself combined strong opinions—ultramontanist in religion, unflaggingly royalist in politics—with gentle behavior. In good part it was from the abbé that Tocqueville acquired his less than optimistic view of human nature, and his core belief that such dignity as men possess is won only through unremitting effort.

When Abbé Lesueur died, Alexis wrote to his brother Édouard: "He always shared our worries, our affections, our concerns, yet nothing tied him to us but his own wish [to be so tied. He was a man] whose every thought, whose every affection, turned on us alone, who seemed to live for us alone." Some thought the abbé had spoiled Alexis; Chateaubriand was of this opinion. The abbé saw great things in him even when the boy was very young, and of course he was not wrong.

Alexis's thoughts about religion derived both from Abbé Lesueur and from his mother, who found in religion her only shelter in a fragile world over which the threat of terror always hovered. Throughout her son's writings, religion is central to the operation of a well-functioning society: its role in providing men with a moral compass can never be gainsaid. In his personal religious views, Alexis went into and out of belief, at times teetering toward agnosticism on the subject of God, at other times yearning to regain a religious center for his own life.

Had Alexis de Tocqueville grown up in a financially more secure family, he might have been a less impressive historian. He was never reduced to having to work for a living, but neither was he ever wealthy on an impressive scale. After his emergence from prison, Hervé de Tocqueville found much of his family wealth greatly depleted by revolutionary skullduggery, in which houses were ransacked, goods stolen, and lands scourged and often expropriated. Alexis witnessed his father's diligent struggle to put his family back on a sound financial basis, which he was able to achieve only after more than a quarter century of careful attention and tactful dealings among disputatious family members. In his son's writing, financial details—taxes, job preferments, exactious luxuries—often play a serious part in crucial political decisions and the momentous events that result from them. Tocqueville knew, for example, that for most people personal profit was more a more persuasive goad to revolution than freedom promised by radical political change. He would later note that "France has always been a country of worried people where everyone has more desires and more vanity than money," a remark that appears to have lost none of its accuracy in our own day.

A royalist spirit reigned *chez* Tocqueville. André Jardin recounts that Tocqueville recalled his family singing, many years after the death of Louis XVI, a song about the sad capture of

the king, which had everyone in the room in tears. The Tocquevilles paid their fealty to the Bourbons and viewed the House of
Orléans as not worthy of their support; Louise de Tocqueville
referred to the Orléanist king Louis-Philippe, contemptuously,
as "Philippe." Of his parents, Alexis's mother was the more or-
thodox in her thinking, the stricter Catholic, and the stronger
royalist.

Alexis's two older brothers appear not to have had any serious influence on him of the kind one sometimes finds older
brothers exerting on the younger. His eldest brother, Hippolyte, eight years older than Alexis, was a French version of the
southern good old boy: a military man, later a political adventurer changing his views almost as frequently as his linen, never
in doubt and usually wrong. In temperament, in cast of mind,
he was the reverse- if not the anti-Alexis. Alexis was closer to
his brother Édouard, who was five years older and—not a difficult state to attain—more thoughtful than Hippolyte. In later
years Édouard wrote on agronomy and was keen to square his
Christian principles with his economic interests and beliefs (he
married a very rich woman). The childless Alexis took a serious
interest in Édouard's sons, their education, and their careers.
He felt an intimacy with Édouard, though there is no evidence
that this closeness had any palpable effect on the development
of his mind. But then genius—and I believe that Tocqueville
qualifies as a genius—is more often influenced by unusual or
accidental than by conventional means.

At some point Louise de Tocqueville settled in Paris,
giving the family a permanent home while her husband trav-

eled between his various prefectural posts. In 1820, now prefect in Metz, Hervé de Tocqueville, out of homesickness for his family, asked that Alexis, the most cerebral of his sons, be sent out to him. At the lycée in Metz, Alexis was instructed in rhetoric by a Monsieur Mougin, who stressed the importance of classical—Greek and Roman—learning, and directed his gifted pupil to the study of history. Alexis would of course become one of the greatest of French historians: a philosophical historian, less concerned with the story of history than with the meaning behind it, whose interests and intellectual emphases were informed by the great classical subjects of ambition, freedom, public virtue, tyranny, and equality. In later years, working up the research for his (never completed) book on the French Revolution, Tocqueville says of a writer on Russia named Hauxthausen that his is a "mind without breadth and without justice." From an early age Alexis de Tocqueville's own mind was in training to acquire both qualities.

Not all that much is known of Tocqueville's life as a student at Metz. At eighteen, he was wounded in a duel—over what exactly is, again, unknown—with a fellow student. He also carried on a romance with a lively young woman named Rosalie Mayle, which lasted five years. Her family was socially beneath his, and a marriage would have been considered a grave misalliance.

During his time in Metz, at the age of sixteen, Tocqueville underwent an intellectual, even more a spiritual, crisis, which he recounted late in life to Anne-Sophie Swetchine, a Russian who kept a salon in Paris and who had become his confidant. Doubt had seeped into his soul through his readings in the prefect's library, where he had encountered the writings of Voltaire, Buffon, and other philosophes. He was devastated by what he encountered in their books. Here is this well-brought-up boy, certain in his belief in the church and respectful toward the monarchy, everything in his world in perfect place, and suddenly he discovers that nothing of what he believes is anywhere near so solid as he thinks—that institutions are not divine or even hallowed by tradition but man-made and thus easily unmade by man; that religion is merely another human invention and a blockade to reason; that science holds all the significant secrets of the universe. "All of a sudden," the fifty-one-year-old Tocqueville writes to Madame Swetchine, "I experience the sensation people talk about who have been through an earthquake, when the ground shakes under their feet, as do the walls around them, the ceilings over their heads, the furniture beneath their hands, all of nature before their eyes. I was seized by the blackest melancholy, then by an extreme disgust with life."

Doubt had the young Alexis by the throat. And doubt was to haunt him, this seemingly most confident of thinkers, all his days—doubt often edging into despair. Tocqueville's was a mind that preyed on itself, sometimes so drastically that he believed he had lost his reason. "There are certain moments," he wrote to his dear friend Gustave de Beaumont, who accompanied him on his journey to America, "when I am so tormented and so little master of myself." He ranked doubt only after death and disease as the third greatest terror in life.

Louis de Kergorlay, another of Tocqueville's dearest friends and also a distant cousin, was someone to whom Alexis regularly brought his doubts. Kergorlay, for whose mind Tocqueville had the greatest regard, was unable to complete any writing of his own, but was an intellectual problem solver of impressive power, and Tocqueville more than once used him in this capacity. Friendship was important to Tocqueville, who wrote of "the beautiful passion of friendship" with Kergorlay in mind, adding that the older he grew "the more I believe that friendship, as I conceived it, can indeed exist and conserve its character, not undoubtedly among all men but among some."

The crisis that Tocqueville underwent at sixteen had the effect of imbuing him early with an unusually measured reading of life's possibilities. He writes to his friend Eugène Stoffels's brother Charles, at a time when the latter was undergoing a bout of deep melancholy, that he knows what Charles is going through, having traveled the same dark road himself. Most people, Alexis goes on to say, hope or fear too much from life. Few people have been continuously happy or unhappy. "Life is therefore neither an excellent nor a very bad thing," he writes, "but, allow me the expression, a *mediocre* thing partaking of both. One must neither expect too much from it, nor fear too much, but attempt to see it as it is, without disgust or enthusiasm, like an inevitable fact, which one has not produced, which one will not cause to stop, and which it is above all a matter of making endurable." Tocqueville reports that he has not come to this view "without great internal conflicts"; nor is he able to hold to it always. But in the final analysis: "Life is neither a pleasure nor a sorrow; it is a serious affair with which we are charged, and toward which our duty is to acquit ourselves as well as possible." This was written in 1831, when Tocqueville was twenty-six.

His crisis in Metz caused Tocqueville to lose his firm religious conviction, much to Abbé Lesueur's disappointment. As he read the philosophes, his confidence in the superiority of the values of his own social class, the French aristocracy, was also shaken. The crisis, however hellish undergoing it at the time must have been for an adolescent boy, was of course ultimately a salutary one, for it turned the young Alexis into a man devoted to the lifelong study of how society works. He would no longer take any social structure or political action for granted: some arrangements might be God-given; God may have set out the larger directions of human destiny; but much remained in the hands of human beings to shape for better or worse. His life would be devoted to attempting to see that it would be shaped for better rather than worse. He was fascinated with the endless interplay of laws, mores, interests, and historical institutions and events that give every society its coloration and finally its character. The character of societies would become his great subject and understanding it in its rich complexity his lifework.

Chapter Two

TRADITION WOULD HAVE had Alexis de Tocqueville, as an aristocrat, take up a military career, as did his two older brothers. But his father had other plans for his youngest and most thoughtful son—specifically, plans for a political career. Under the restoration government of Louis XVIII and later his brother Charles X, which followed the final defeat of Napoleon, one had to be forty years old to become a member of the National Assembly. In the meantime, Alexis would take up law, a career he entered with no great enthusiasm. After completing the requirements for a legal education, in 1828, at the age of twenty-two, he was, through his father's influence, appointed a *juge auditeur*, assigned to the court at Versailles.

The French court system was a hierarchy organized by seniority. The president of the court, the presiding judge, was at its top, with a vice president and seven other judges following in order of rank; there were also three public prosecutors and, at the bottom, four *juges auditeurs*. The *juges auditeurs* were unpaid, and their responsibilities ranged from those of a glorified clerk to conducting investigations, from defending briefs to sometimes sitting as surrogate judges.

The law courts opened each year with the *juges auditeurs* giving a speech on a general subject. Tocqueville drew the subject of dueling. André Jardin reports that in his speech the young Alexis made the point that the law could never hope to stop dueling so long as the national mores favored it—that is, so long as personal honor continued to be valued above the penalty for taking another man's life. Holding that the practice was unlikely to cease until such time as religion could successfully admonish men not to settle their disputes by violence, Tocqueville argued: "Remake the man before you remake the citizen.... And then you will have effective laws." Early in his career though this dueling speech was, it is a very characteristic, a very (one might say) Tocquevillian, performance. Laws without mores to reinforce them will generally lose meaning and hence significance.

Tocqueville had no natural talent for the practice of law. He lacked the gift of easy eloquence—a gift that would elude him even more importantly in his later career as a parliamentary politician. Restrained, aloof, caustic, his bearing was thought cold. Paintings and drawings of him from this period show a thin-lipped, rather disapproving mouth. The problem of temperamental coldness was compounded by his being unable to concern himself with what he considered trivial matters; a thoroughgoing intellectual elitist, he did not have it in him to feign an interest in people he thought mediocre.

In law, Tocqueville was less taken with the abstract application of legal principles than with the rendering of moral judgments, a point that foreshadows the moral tone behind his mature writings. He became slightly contemptuous of the legal profession, remarking at one point on "the circumspect and shriveled souls hidden under black robes." His performance at the court of Versailles was so lackluster that he was passed over for promotion to deputy prosecutor; and some four years later, when he left the legal profession after returning from his famous trip to North America, he had yet to earn a sou from it.

The profit, though, was in the friendships Tocqueville made among his fellow *juges auditeurs,* especially that with Gustave de Beaumont. A man with literary talent and skill as a painter, Beaumont, like Alexis, was an aristocrat, who would later marry the granddaughter of Lafayette. Of the *petite noblesse,* Beaumont's family was also bred to responsibility: his father, Comte Jules de Beaumont, served as mayor of the town of Sarthe, in the west of France. With a wide forehead and an appealingly open face, sociable and at home in all company, Gustave de Beaumont was large and robust, good-natured and easygoing, and very different temperamentally from the introspective and guarded Tocqueville. Yet the rapport between the two men was immediate and their devotion to each other would be lifelong.

In *Allemands et Français* Heinrich Heine wrote about their friendship during a later phase: "What Tocqueville lacks in feeling, his friend M. de Beaumont possesses it in overabundance; and these two inseparables whom we always see joined together, in their travels, in their publications, in the Chamber of Deputies, perfect each other superbly. One the severe thinker, the other the man of gushing feeling, go together like a bottle of vinegar and a bottle of oil." This salad-dressing simile perhaps overstates Tocqueville's coldness, his severity, his detachment—a point evidenced by the depth of his friendship with Gustave de Beaumont.

Although Beaumont was three years older, his own political development was roughly congruent with Tocqueville's: in each man, a lingering loyalty to the class into which he was born was gradually being eroded by an awakening liberalism. Together they attempted to read and think their way out of the quandary in which a time of great political instability had landed them.

Forming a two-man study group, Tocqueville and Beaumont together read English history and political economy. They attended the lectures on French civilization of François Guizot, given in Paris in 1828, lectures emphasizing the relentless progress of the middle and lower classes that made up the third estate—the nobility and the clergy constituting, respectively, the first and second estates—toward establishing equality in France. In Guizot's interpretation, the theme underlying history was progress, and progress meant the elimination of privilege and the spread of power among all. Tocqueville and Beaumont—but Tocqueville especially—were swept away by the comprehensiveness of Guizot, who understood that all man's works, from his political institutions through his laws, his art, his intellectual constructs, and the influence of foreign countries on him, were grist for the mill of history.

History itself meanwhile forced Tocqueville's and Beaumont's hand with the advent of the July Revolution in France. That revolution was brought on by the deep ineptitude of Charles X, who, after appointing an unacceptably royalist roster of cabinet ministers, forced through what came to be known as the famous four ordinances: one suppressing freedom of the press, a second dissolving the Chamber of Deputies, a third modifying electoral laws in favor of the king, and the fourth fixing a new election earlier than was planned. The result was a coup d'état. Barricades went up in the streets of Paris; and after three days of insurrection, from July 28–30, the game was over. Withdrawing his ordinances did not save Charles X, whose carriage, mud spattering the Bourbon coat of arms on its door, departed Paris early in August—a sight Alexis de Tocqueville, with richly complicated feelings, witnessed in person.

The successor to Charles X was the duc d'Orléans, who became King Louis-Philippe. Monarchy in France, as Tocqueville's cousin Chateaubriand exclaimed, was "no longer a religion." In choosing Louis-Philippe and discharging Charles X, the French had, in effect, chosen a bourgeois over an aristocratic monarchy. The king was accepted only by his agreeing to the demands of the third estate as a condition of his ascendancy. The monarchy set in motion by the July revolution was a constitutional monarchy: no longer did all power flow from the sovereign; rather, the sovereign, for the first time in French history, served at the discretion of the French people. Kingship was no longer hereditary; the legislative chambers had quite as much power to make laws as the king, Catholicism ceased to be the official state religion, and suffrage was to be considerably extended. Even the name Louis-Philippe I, instead of Philippe VII, suggested a break with the past, a new deal of sorts.

The problem in this for Tocqueville and for Beaumont was that Louis-Philippe's family, the house of Orléans, was always viewed with the strongest suspicion by their families, which held firm allegiance to the Bourbons. The Orléans had identified, if not altogether sided, with the French Revolution, even if Louis-Philippe's father had himself eventually been guillotined during the Terror. Louis-Philippe in effect served as king of the revolution, which now meant as king, too, of the wealthy bourgeois, whose rise in power accompanied his accession to the throne.

To set the seal on its acquisition of power, the new government asked for an oath of loyalty from those who served it—including the *juges auditeurs,* Tocqueville and Beaumont among them. One had to stand on a platform and take this oath in public. Tocqueville felt that the political crudity of Charles X had deservedly brought him down, and though his own position was tending more and more toward the liberal, family pressure did not make his taking the oath easy. Hervé de Tocqueville resigned from office when Louis-Philippe became king. Family and friends instructed Alexis to forgo taking the oath. But such career prospects as he had was at stake, and so he and Beaumont both, in the end, gave in. "I have at last sworn the oath," Tocqueville wrote to Mary Mottley, the Englishwoman he was then courting and would one day marry. "My conscience does not reproach me, but I am still deeply wounded and I will count this day among the most unhappy of my life.... I am at war with myself, this is a new state for me, and it horrifies me."

In the event, Tocqueville found it easier to pledge allegiance to Louis-Philippe than actually to serve him. The time seemed propitious to remove himself, if only temporarily, from the scene of government. He and Beaumont came up with the ingenious notion of traveling to North America to study the new republic's penal system, said to provide a model of the way of the future. In France prisons were the subject of much criticism. French prisons were typically dungeons, storage houses for criminals, and hence a breeding ground for more crime. In America penal institutions were more concerned with the rehabilitation and reform of their inmates. So the notion of sending these two young magistrates to discover how it was done in the United States had a certain appeal to the new government. Much negotiation about who would pay for such a trip was carried on; Tocqueville and Beaumont, in their eagerness to be out of the country, had originally agreed to pay their own expenses, and when they later hoped to have the government pick up their bills, they were unsuccessful. But the government did finally agree to allow Tocqueville and Beaumont an eighteen-month leave of absence to visit and report on the treatment of criminals in America.

In a letter written to Charles Stoffels quoted by André Jardin, one that reads like a man talking to himself, Tocqueville estimates the potential value of his planned trip to America: "In itself the trip has taken you [he means himself] out of the most commonplace class. The knowledge you have gained in such a celebrated nation has separated you from the crowd. You know exactly what a vast republic is, why it is practicable in one place, impracticable in another. All aspects of public administration have been examined one by one. When you return to France you certainly feel strength that you didn't have when you left. If the time is favorable, some sort of publication on your part can alert the public to your existence and turn the attention of the [newly forming political] parties to you."

Alexis de Tocqueville was always a careful caretaker of his own career, and the trip to America, ostensibly to study prisons, was what we should today call an extremely good career move. Resulting in *Democracy in America,* the trip would be the making of his reputation, turning him, for the remainder of his life, into an important thinker throughout Europe and everywhere else among people who pondered the complex problems of government.

Chapter Three

Tocqueville and Beaumont left for North America on April 2, 1831. They sailed from Le Havre on an American ship with a crew of eighteen and 163 passengers, just thirty-one of them (including Tocqueville and Beaumont) having cabins.

The young commissioners, as they were now officially known, brought clothes for all weather, including greatcoats, all manner of shoes, and duds to be worn when among what in America passed for fashionable society; they also packed many little notebooks, fowling pieces for hunting, and (for Beaumont) a flute, pencils, and a sketchbook. They carried more than seventy letters of introduction to various officials and important persons. Abbé Lesueur, now eighty, gave his fallen-away, still dear pupil Alexis a prayer book, with an inscription predicting that they would one day meet in heaven.

Owing to rough weather, Tocqueville was seasick the first

few days out. On an earlier voyage to Sicily, traveling with his brother Édouard, Tocqueville had sailed through a storm of such violence that he and his fellow passengers thought it might end all their lives. Without religious confidence as a life preserver, he felt acutely the uncaring strength of nature and the defenselessness of human beings when confronted by what he called the *toute-puissance divine*. In *Democracy in America*, he recounted visiting an abandoned island in New York on which a man and his wife had once lived but which had now been returned to nature: "For some time I silently admired the resourcefulness of nature and the weakness of man, and when at last I was obliged to leave that enchanted place, I muttered to myself sadly, 'How astonishing! Ruins already!'" Tocqueville would remark again on the sheer terrifying force of nature when traversing the dense forests of upper Michigan, underscoring the pitiful weakness of men next to the power of nature. The theme recurs in his writing: the force of nature is powerful, the construct of civilization fragile.

The crossing took thirty-eight days, a few days longer than usual for an Atlantic voyage. The boredom quotient, at least for the first half of the trip, was exceedingly high. The ship's full passenger list is missing, so the names of all Tocqueville and Beaumont's fellow travelers are not known. What is known is that Tocqueville and Beaumont worked those Americans onboard for contributions to their scant knowledge about the new republic that was their destination. Among the passengers were an Englishman who had been in the House of Commons and Peter Schermerhorn, of the well-established Dutch New

York merchant family, originally ship chandlers, whose members had gone into real estate speculation and development. A young American woman, a Miss Edwards, helped them with their English, which was less proficient than they had thought, and a Mr. Palmer provided further help in this line. ("Our most urgent need," Beaumont wrote to his parents, "is to speak English well.") Tocqueville won a shooting contest, in which the target was a barrel set loose in the sea.

When not at meals or exercising on deck, they studied in their small cabin, reading the existing literature on penal institutions and the books they had brought along on the American economy and American political organization. (Later, in America, on the advice of a well-educated lawyer, they would acquire a copy of *The Federalist* and of Kent's *Commentaries on American Law,* both of which proved greatly useful.) Slowly, they began to formulate their preliminary thoughts on the country they were about to visit.

One of the small astonishments of this arduous trip is that these two young men, so strikingly different in temperament, seem never to have tired of each other's constant company. From America, Beaumont wrote to his mother: "Tocqueville is a really distinguished man. He has high-minded ideas and great nobility of soul; the better I know him, the more I like him." Tocqueville spoke often about their good fortune in finding each other and later wrote to Beaumont to tell him that he was "the only man in the world on whose judgment I can lean with confidence."

Evidence from their letters and diaries shows that Tocqueville and Beaumont had, from the outset, larger plans than the production of a study of prison arrangements in America. Before his departure, Tocqueville wrote to Eugène Stoffels: "We are leaving with the intention of examining in detail and as scientifically as possible all the mechanisms of this vast American society about which everyone talks and no one knows. And if events allow us the time, we expect to bring back the elements of a *bon ouvrage,* or at least of a new work; for nothing exists on this subject." This last is an exaggeration: what Tocqueville meant to say was that nothing really good existed on life in the young American republic.

Beaumont, meanwhile, wrote to his father that "we are meditating great projects." Allowing that their first responsibility was to their report on prisons, he went on to remark that he and Tocqueville would also "be visiting [America's] inhabitants, its cities, its institutions, its customs; we shall get to know the mechanism of its republican government." Would it not be a fine thing, he goes on to ask, to produce "a book which would give an exact conception of the American people, would paint its character in bold strokes, would analyze its social conditions and would rectify so many opinions which are erroneous on this point?" From New York, Beaumont wrote to his brother Jules that "we are laying the foundations of a great work which should make our reputations someday."

As we now know, this great work would make chiefly Tocqueville's reputation. Beaumont wrote about the grand project in the first person plural, but, in the end, the "we" turned into "I," the "I" belonging to Alexis de Tocqueville, whose name would light up skies with its aura of shimmering political intelligence while the cheerful and good-hearted Beaumont would remain a subsidiary player, a second violin, unknown outside France except to those who have studied Tocqueville. (Beaumont would join Tocqueville as a member of the Chamber of Deputies through most of the 1840s, would serve as the French ambassador to London and to Vienna, and would edit Tocqueville's posthumously published works; but his fame is mainly linked to that of Tocqueville.)

The two commissioners landed in Newport, Rhode Island, on May 8, 1831. They straightaway took a steamship to New York City, where they alighted three days later. There they discovered that an announcement had preceded them, printed in the New York *Mercantile Advertiser*, and subsequently reprinted in other papers in Boston, Philadelphia, Baltimore, and elsewhere, that two young French magistrates had arrived to study the American penal system.

In New York, much to their pleased surprise, they were greeted as dignitaries, officials of weight and seriousness, minor celebrities even, and were taken up by the best society of the day. This is all the more interesting because so many foreign visitors to America returned to Europe to write critically about the country; this was especially true of the English, most famously of Mrs. Frances Trollope (in *Domestic Manners of the Americans*, 1832) and, later, of Charles Dickens (in *Martin Chuzzlewit* and elsewhere), but also of lesser figures. Anti-Americanism in those days had a chiefly snobbish, not yet a political, tone.

At the time of Tocqueville and Beaumont's arrival, the population of the United States was roughly 13 million people (along with 2 million slaves), divided among twenty-four states. Development beyond the Mississippi River was nearly nonexistent. Much of upper Michigan and of Ohio was still wilderness. President Andrew Jackson was in the final year of his first term. Abraham Lincoln was twenty-two; Emerson, twenty-eight; Thoreau, fourteen; Melville, twelve. The population of New York City was 120,000. The country, though no longer in its infancy, had scarcely advanced much beyond its childhood.

Everywhere Tocqueville and Beaumont found fluidity, movement, flux, which didn't make the job of capturing the character of American society any easier. As Tocqueville wrote to his friend Ernest de Chabrol: "Picture to yourself, my dear friend, if you can, a society which comprises all the nations of the world—English, French, German: people differing from one another in language, in beliefs, in opinions; in a word, a society possessing no roots, no memories, no prejudices, no routine, no common ideas, no national character, yet with a happiness a hundred times greater than ours."

On first impression at least, for Tocqueville this happiness was highly qualified by what he took to be the chauvinistic, less than penetrating outlook of the Americans he met in New York. Always hard on people he felt were unthoughtful, he couldn't bear to be in their company, no matter what their social class or nationality. (Later in his trip, he scored off the French consul in New Orleans, for example, as a man who "had one of those egotistical intelligences which speaks but does not converse and which finds pleasure in the sight of its own thoughts.") He felt Americans were for the most part without personal distinction or elegance of manner. An exception, met in New York, was the Swiss-born Albert Gallatin, former secretary of the treasury under Jefferson, a man of deep culture who could talk with him and Beaumont in faultless French.

Better educated on average than Europeans though Americans might be, there was nonetheless "something both vulgar and disagreeably uncultivated" about them, or so Tocqueville felt on first impression. He had never before encountered a country so middle-class—he was struck by the fact that the governor of the state of New York lived in a boardinghouse—yet he sensed that American ambition did not go much beyond self-interest, which is to say mere moneymaking. These, as noted, were first impressions, and they would be altered, in ways large and small, during the course of the next nine months.

The entire length of Tocqueville and Beaumont's visit would be 271 days, with another fifteen days spent traveling in Canada, and a fair portion of their time was wasted slogging through forests, on snow-laden roads, or bogged down in icy rivers on malfunctioning steamships. In this limited time, their observations and insights, a combination of both men's thoughts eventually finely ground through the mind of Tocqueville, would result in a classic of political science and political philosophy: "the best book ever written on democracy and the best book ever written on America," according to Harvey C. Mansfield and Delba Winthrop, in their introduction to their translation into English of *Democracy in America* (2000).

Intelligent as Tocqueville was, and good-hearted as Beaumont was, neither man was without Old World snobbery. Tocqueville reported to his dear Abbé Lesueur that the preparation and serving of food in America "represented the infancy of art: the vegetables and fish before the meat, the oysters for dessert. In a word, complete barbarism." They both feared being drunk under the table owing to the vast number of toasts offered at several dinners given in their honor. Beaumont always made a note of how wretched the performance of music was in American homes; the piano playing and singing of his hostesses left him dangling between excruciating boredom and deep distaste. Tocqueville described much of the singing as "howling" and "caterwauling." Beaumont thought a good bed "unheard of in America." Both had an eye for pretty American girls, though they noted that young women in the United States were without the arts of flirtation and cultivated guile; the light, ironic touch was entirely missing from their relations with men. Early in the trip an unpleasant note of social slumming crept into some of Tocqueville's and Beaumont's letters home to family and friends.

Tocqueville and Beaumont traveled through seventeen of the twenty-four American states that then existed, covering roughly 7,300 miles of terrain. Beginning in New York City, they journeyed upstate for a nine-day visit to the prison at Sing Sing, which contained 900 prisoners watched over by thirty guards. The prison operated under the Auburn system, which imposed full-time silence on the prisoners, with corporeal punishment (whipping) for any violations of strictly coded behavior.

Because of the great reputation of *Democracy in America*, the tendency is to assume that Tocqueville was omniscient, a man on whom nothing was lost. But the fact is that there was much of significance he simply wasn't interested in: the steamboat, early industrialization, material progress of all sorts, general economic trends. His chief interest was social and political observation—how people lived and what they believed, and how the machinery of their government was designed and worked. Had he been interested in everything, he might not have written so remarkable a book.

After their tour of Sing Sing, Tocqueville and Beaumont returned to New York City, where they made a connection for a trip to Albany by steamboat—a steamboat called the *North America* that was, while the Frenchmen were aboard, in a race with other boats, causing it to miss the stop for West Point, where Tocqueville and Beaumont had hoped to visit to the military academy. Following two days in Albany, seat of the state government, they repaired to the Finger Lakes region, traveling by horseback and stagecoach to Auburn and Buffalo. Along the way, they spotted many Indians—here of the Iroquois tribe—as they would throughout their trip. The Indian Removal Act, forcing Indians to move westward, had been passed in 1830 with strong support from President Jackson. Beaumont's sympathies were instantly and fully engaged by the plight of the Indians, and he stated his desire to devote all his intellectual energy to studying them. Tocqueville admired the aristocratic grandeur of bearing of the Indians, even in their degraded state, but recognized that they were already a doomed people.

From Buffalo, then thought to be a city with a great industrial future, they proceeded to Cleveland and thence to Detroit, where they stayed a single day. Beaumont, worried about Tocqueville's health, was much concerned about their moving on too quickly. He needn't have worried; he couldn't have stopped his partner if he had wished. Despite all appearances of physical delicacy, Tocqueville had great inner stamina, though one day, while hunting, he attempted to swim what his nearsighted vision led him to think was a narrow stream, and nearly drowned.

On July 23, they set out, on horseback, on the Saginaw Trail, to Saginaw, Michigan. A rough trail, which became even harsher because of relentless swarms of mosquitoes, made the trip a nightmare; an Indian guide with whom they could not communicate was their sole company. They did, however, encounter some frontier families, whose courageous self-sufficiency much impressed Tocqueville. He would later write up this part of the journey in an essay-travelogue he called *Quinze jours au désert,* or "A Fortnight in the Wilderness."

After returning to Detroit, they boarded another steamboat, the *Superior,* for a trip into the upper Great Lakes, bound for Mackinac Island, Sault Sainte Marie, and Green Bay, Wisconsin. Finding themselves this far north, they decided to visit Canada. They made stops in Montreal and Quebec, observing French culture as it had taken root in the new world. On this leg of their journey, they also saw Niagara Falls. Tocqueville was awed by its power, as he invariably was with scenes of the magnificent unheeding force of nature.

Tocqueville compared the solitude he found in the American wilderness to that he had known in the Swiss Alps, though he found the American version of a different order. In America, he wrote, "the only feelings one experiences in journeying through these flowered wildernesses where, as in Milton's *Paradise,* all is prepared to receive man, are a tranquil admiration, a vague distaste for civilized life, a sweet and melancholy emotion, a sort of wild instinct which makes one reflect with sadness that soon this delightful solitude will be completely altered [by further incursions of white Europeans]."

Yet at other other times he noted "the feeling of isolation and abandonment, which had seemed so heavy to us in the mid-Atlantic, [and which] I have found more strong and poignant perhaps in the solitude of the New World." At sea at least the horizon suggested hope; but the immensity of the American forest suggested only more, endlessly more, of the same: "You can travel thousands of leagues in its shade and you advance always without seeming to change your place." At night Tocqueville's contemplation of this relentless immensity resulted in something very near sheer terror.

Throughout their trip, Tocqueville and Beaumont were fortunate to meet the men they did, men they grilled about the political institutions and social *moeurs* of Americans. Tocqueville carefully recorded the results of these interrogations in his many notebooks, which he referred to as his *cahiers portatifs.* John Canfield Spencer in New York; Joel Poinsett in South Carolina; one Father Mullon, whom they met aboard a steamship; John Latrobe; Charles Carroll (said to be the wealthiest man in Maryland); and many others were pumped for their views about American attitudes toward religion, inheritance, tax and other laws, jury trials, the press, slavery, and much more. The flow of useful information they obtained speaks both to the kindness of their American interlocutors and to the charm of the two young Frenchman in winning them over.

Boston, crucial in so many ways for the book Tocqueville was to write, was next on their itinerary, and provided an especially rich lode of such respondents. Here they met John Quincy Adams, then only two years out of the presidency; Daniel Webster; Edward Everett; Josiah Quincy Jr. (president of Harvard); the publisher George Ticknor; and (most useful of all for their researches) the Reverend Jared Sparks, who had a large collection of the papers of George Washington and was himself a mine of information on the complexities of American political and social life.

Boston also provided a more elevated intellectual atmosphere than New York City, causing Tocqueville to revise his view, first arrived at in New York, that Americans were chiefly interested in accumulating wealth. They stayed three and a half weeks in Boston. The model of New England town government gave him an indispensable entrée into the motivating political forces and participatory nature of American government. In Boston, too, they met Franz Lieber, himself a careful foreign student of America, who would one day translate *Democracy in America* into German.

In Boston, on September 9, 1831, Tocqueville learned of the death of his beloved Abbé Lesueur, which dropped him into deep sadness. Soon after, he and Beaumont were informed by the French Ministry of Justice that the length of their visit would have to be shortened.

Throughout the trip, Tocqueville and Beaumont, along with the diaries and self-addressed memoranda they accumulated, sent letters to their friends and respective families in France. In these letters they set out their observations on America—observations that Tocqueville would later call on when he began the composition of his book. They also wrote to friends and family for information of which they were ignorant on intricate points of contemporary French government and for information about the political affairs of the day. Tocqueville's book may have been about America, but, as many have noted, it was written with the French as its ideal audience. Tocqueville was always a comparatist, writing about the United States with England and especially France never far from his mind. "The mind," he wrote to his father from America, "becomes clear only by comparison."

Hartford and Philadelphia were their next stops. As they had missed West Point in New York, so in Connecticut they missed Yale. That seems a pity; one recalls Santayana writing eighty or so years later about the spirit of muscular Christianity at Yale, which combined religion and the need for business success: precisely the kind of observation Tocqueville would have approved. Instead they visited the main penitentiary in Connecticut. They had also visited prisons in Boston, and were most impressed with the city's reform-school institution for the young, which was run along roughly democratic lines.

In Philadelphia, though, Tocqueville and Beaumont found the centerpiece of their study of the penitentiary system. There the influence of the Quakers in prison reform was on display in a solitary-centered system in which, for a long spell, there was no social intercourse among prisoners, and labor was allowed only late in a prisoner's confinement. Prisoners were left alone for long stretches with only a Bible and their own sins to contemplate. At Eastern State Penitentiary, in Philadelphia, Tocqueville interviewed a number of prisoners to get their reaction to this system: most, desolated by loneliness, were eager to get back to working with other prisoners. But American prisons had begun to bore the young French commissioners. "We always see the same thing [in them]," Beaumont wrote to his family.

After two weeks in Philadelphia, they plunged into the South, beginning with nearby Baltimore. Here they had their first view of slavery, which affected Beaumont, always immediately responsive to suffering, with particular force. It may have been in Baltimore that Beaumont first tentatively decided to sheer off and concentrate his own later intellectual efforts on slavery, the Indian question, and other minorities in America. (With his intrinsic sympathy for the underdog, he would also later write about the Irish.) He and Tocqueville were taken to the cell of a slave so abused by his master that the man went out of his mind, and spent his days howling in fear and fury.

By November they traveled from Baltimore to Pittsburgh, on a steamboat that was wrecked in the Ohio River, near Wheeling, West Virginia, giving Tocqueville his second experience of nearly drowning. Escaping the wreckage, they embarked on yet another ship for the burgeoning city of Cincinnati. Here Tocqueville had interesting talks with Salmon P. Chase, later secretary of the treasury under Lincoln and chief justice of the United States; an intelligent lawyer named John McClean (about the American electoral and jury systems); and Timothy Walker, a recent graduate of Harvard College who would go on to a brilliant career in the law. Tocqueville was alerted by these men of the danger that resided in majority rule—of what he would later famously refer to as the tyranny of the majority, or the despotism of democracy. He also came to understand a central fact about slavery in America: considering the prosperity in the free state of Ohio next to the stagnant conditions obtaining in the slave state of Kentucky, he concluded that "man is not made for servitude," and that whenever he subjects other men to this condition, everyone, master and slave, suffers.

After a four-day stay in Ohio, Beaumont and Tocqueville set out for New Orleans. Because of particularly harsh winter weather, river travel was made impossible and they were bogged down for ten days between Nashville and Memphis. Tocqueville, whose weakened lungs always put him at risk, took ill from tromping in the snow, and they rested in a drafty log cabin. He soon recovered, and was well enough to set off on another steamer, on Christmas Day, for New Orleans. Among his and Beaumont's fellow passengers were a bereft and bedraggled group of Choctaw Indians and a Virginian named Sam Houston, who would soon establish his fame as first president and then governor of Texas.

Tocqueville and Beaumont arrived in New Orleans on New Year's Day, 1832, and were able to spend only three days there. Their chief guide to the city was the French consul, a Monsieur Guillemain, who filled them in on the social and political organization of the city—a city distinguished from all other large American cities by its heavily French and Catholic population.

Because of the earlier word from the French government that their mission had been shortened, they traveled rapidly by stagecoach through the southern states—Alabama, Georgia, and the Carolinas—to their final destination, Washington. They had to pass up Charleston. They journeyed more than 1,000 miles in twelve days, and missed pausing to consider in any detail the Deep South, with its plantation culture, which is really to say its slavery culture.

Their trip ended with a visit of two and a half weeks to Washington, still in its early phase of development. They had a forty-five-minute interview with Andrew Jackson, which, though scarcely more than a perfunctory social call, nonetheless left them unimpressed. Jackson seemed to them little more than a military man without either culture or intellectual curiosity. They visited both houses of Congress, from which, similarly, they departed feeling less than exalted: the level of discourse, here, too, struck them as deplorably low. Sadly, they failed to meet James Madison, who was then eighty-one and easily the greatest political theorist of the day. Back in France, Tocqueville read Madison's essays in *The Federalist*, with much benefit for his own book.

On February 20, 1832, back aboard the same ship, the

Havre, that had brought them over, Tocqueville and Beaumont sailed for France, uncertain about what they would find in a volatile French political scene; about what precisely they would do with their lives; and about what use they would make of their vast quantity of notes, pamphlets, diaries, self-addressed memoranda, and other material. All they knew for certain was that they would write up the report on the prison system in America, the ostensible purpose of the trip.

Along with the factual information he had stored up, Tocqueville also acquired a few central truths that would serve him as a political philosopher. "The more I see of this country," he had written to his father fairly early in his visit to America, "the more I admit myself penetrated with this truth: that there is nothing absolute in the theoretical value of political institutions, and that their efficiency depends almost always on the original circumstances and the social condition of the people to whom they are applied." In other words, the young Tocqueville already knew that practical experience and customs (*moeurs*) take precedence over ideas and laws. But with his habitual taste for complexity, he needed to know in what proportion this is so: "That is the great problem about which one cannot reflect too much. I believe that customs have an existence permanent and independent of the laws." He would work out the proper proportion and much more besides when, back in France, he was able to find the time and composure to sit down to the composition of his great book.

Chapter Four

Toward the end of his visit to America, Alexis de Tocqueville wrote to his father: "I have thought a good deal about what might be written about America. To try to present a complete picture of the Union would be an enterprise absolutely impracticable for a man who has passed but a year in this immense country. I believe, moreover, that such a work would be as boring as it would be uninstructive. One might be able, on the other hand, by selecting the topics, to present only those subjects having a more or less direct relation to our [France's] social and political state.... There's the plan: but will I have the time and discover in myself the ability to carry it out? That's the question. There is, besides, one consideration always present in my mind; I shall write what I think or nothing; and all truth is not palatable [*bonne à dire*]."

How characteristic a passage! It displays in one swoop Tocqueville's ambition (never negligible), his dubiety (usually present), and his insistence on his own integrity (of all his qualities, the one never in doubt). He was deeply worried about writing his great work. Leaving America after just nine months' stay, Tocqueville noted that it would require a visit of at least two years to be able to write about the country in a persuasive way. But his ambition never slackened. He understood what composing an important book on a great subject would do for his career. Although aristocracy might be on its way out, the mind still counted for something in France. But how to begin? How to cook, cut up, and make palatable this great elephant of a subject?

First, Tocqueville had to confront his own restlessness and what, it appears reasonable to call it, his depression. Part of the depression was owing to the political situation in France, which seemed to him even worse now than before his departure for America. "I am afflicted, disgusted, almost *honteux* [ashamed] at the state I find my country in," he wrote to Eugène Stoffels. Earlier, to Beaumont, he wrote: "Truly, the world of politics is a foul pit." Since his own plan was for a career in politics, he found this state of affairs, to put it gently, discouraging.

Then the news came through that Gustave de Beaumont had been dismissed from his post as a court's magistrate. In pressing for a leave of absence to travel to America, Beaumont had apparently made enemies, who now wished to get at him by assigning him a case he had no inclination (and no strict duty) to take on. While arguing why he shouldn't have been asked to undertake this case—he was to prosecute an alleged slanderer who happened to be a Legitimist, a man of Beaumont's own party—he was summarily fired, a dismissal he first learned about, humiliatingly, in the press. When Tocqueville, too, learned about it, he handed in his own resignation, striking, as he was very good at doing, the high note of injured dignity: "Long bound by intimate friendship to the man who has thus just been discharged, whose opinions I share and of whose conduct I approve, I feel bound to associate myself voluntarily with his fate, and abandon with him a career where service and uprightness are unable to forestall an undeserved disgrace."

Meanwhile, Tocqueville's friend Louis de Kergorlay was caught plotting with the Duchesse de Berry and Bourbon counterrevolutionaries, who wished to restore a Bourbon monarchy in France, replacing the Orléanist administration of Louis-Philippe. Kergorlay was eventually found not guilty; Tocqueville, serving as his second attorney, spoke on his behalf, arguing that his friend was acting in what he thought his country's best interest. But the entire business suggested further revolutionary turmoil, and Tocqueville was further demoralized by the episode.

All this could not have done much to assuage what appeared to be Tocqueville's writer's block. That dread affliction can have various causes; in Tocqueville's case surely more than a single cause was entailed. Not least was the vastness of the project. Before taking it on, he had to pass along to Beaumont the main work of the actual writing out of their report on the American prison systems. Tocqueville did further research on French prison ships, supplied many of the notes for the study, and served as its general editor. But he evidently felt he had shirked his duty, and wrote to Beaumont: "I have not done anything, or as little as possible. My mind is in lethargy, and I absolutely do not know when it will awaken." The report, titled *Du système pénitentiaire aux États-Unis et de son application en France*, was published in January 1833, and won the Montyon Prize of the Académie Française, of 3,000 francs. "All I contributed were my observations and a few notes," Tocqueville told a correspondent, "M. de Beaumont was really the sole author." He may have overstated the case when he allowed that his contributions to it were so minimal, for Beaumont and he talked a great deal about prisons and traded ideas on the subject from the outset.

A year had passed, and Tocqueville still had not plunged into his book on America. Whether because of the dithering caused by writer's block or because he still thought himself ill prepared for his subject, Tocqueville, ever the comparatist, felt that he ought to investigate democracy in England, where he betook himself for a five-week tour beginning in August 1833. He had been in England before, but now he traveled with all the issues, questions, and problems posed by democratic government that his trip to America had placed in the forefront of his mind.

Reading the notes Tocqueville kept on this trip to England, one discovers his preoccupations of the moment. Centralization of governmental duties and of law is primary; and here he finds that the English are fortunate in contriving to have arrangements much more decentralized, much less uniform generally, than those of the French. The role of religion in England, which has an established church, but with many other religious sects flourishing unharmed around it, seems to Tocqueville another English advantage. When religion was attacked, as it was during the French Revolution, everyone knew that it was the Catholic Church and clergy who were under attack; in England whenever religion came under attack, he noted the attack is much more diffuse, more general than particular, and therefore less direct and harmful.

On this English trip, Tocqueville was much taken, too, with the difference between the English and French aristocracies. In his notes he makes the crucial point that the French aristocracy can be entered only by birth, whereas the English aristocracy is open to fortune—one can, in other words, buy or marry one's way in: one can thus become an English gentleman but never a French *gentilhomme*. The French aristocracy, being more unitary, was also much more open to attack, whereas the English aristocracy, not sharing a unified body of opinion, was much less easily attacked. Tocqueville predicted, to himself, that the English aristocracy would one day disappear, but much more slowly than the French. Only now, nearly 200 years later, is this particular prediction beginning to come true.

Soon after he arrived in England, Tocqueville paid a visit to the House of Lords, a less purely ceremonial institution in 1833 than it has subsequently become. Of the scene he found he reports that "there was nothing pompous, but a general air of good manners, an easy good taste and, so to say, an *aroma* of aristocracy." Despite knowing that aristocracy was on its way out, he never really lost his taste for the grandeur of aristocratic style. "It is not necessary," he wrote, "to attach too much importance to this loss [of aristocracy]; but it is permissible to regret it." He ends by describing the great English military hero Lord Wellington, conqueror of Napoleon, who turned out to have been a nervous and ineffective speaker.

In contrast to Wellington, Tocqueville writes of a man, self-described as "a worker in the lower grades of industry," who, speaking on behalf of England's commitment to Polish independence, "carried [me] away, body and soul, by the irresistible torrent of his oratory, so strongly was I affected by the real warmth of his feelings and the energy of his delivery." Aristocrat though Tocqueville was, he could also, in thought and in feeling, slip outside the aristocracy and rise above it when the occasion required. As J. P. Mayer, one of his early interpreters, writes, "He has never served a class, he always upheld the sanctity of the human soul, so infinitely threatened by the modern State structure which he analyzed in its historical beginnings."

Tocqueville's trip to England had the salutary effect of breaking his writer's block. By October 1833 he had installed himself in the attic in his family's house in Paris on the rue de Verneuil and set to work in earnest. The immensity of his materials, not to speak of all he still needed to know, doubtless contributed to his earlier hesitation. Tocqueville was a relentless organizer of his own research, a note-taker and journal-keeper and a diarist of his own reading; and his first task was to organize his own research, which he soon enough did.

From the American legation in Paris, Tocqueville hired two

young men, Theodore Sedgwick III and Francis J. Lippitt. This is perhaps the earliest recorded use of (in effect) graduate research assistants. He used the two very differently. Both were assigned to bring him books and documents from the legation, but he used Sedgwick to sound out his own thoughts about the complexities of American life, and he and Tocqueville, in the words of George Wilson Pierson, "became fast friends." Lippitt he held at such a distance that the young man wasn't aware that Tocqueville spoke English. "He was the most reticent man I ever met," Lippitt wrote many years later. Only twice did Tocqueville ever actually speak to Lippitt, who also didn't know that he was writing a book on America. That Tocqueville could command such coldness is itself an indication of the *hauteur* of which he was capable.

A writer who was almost continually formulating and re-formulating his ideas, Tocqueville kept something akin to a running commentary on his own writing. He searched for what he called his *idée mère,* or the central or fructifying idea from which many other ideas and observations would be generated. He made and changed outlines. He began with the facts learned on his visit to America; from these facts he deduced his ideas, and the ideas in their turn required that he learn fresh facts, many of these acquired from his extensive reading. "So far as I know," he wrote in the introduction to *Democracy in America,* "I never gave in to the temptation to tailor facts to ideas rather than to adapt ideas to facts." In a letter of 1836 to John Stuart Mill, Tocqueville described his method—if method it be—of composition:

I am never precisely sure where I am going or whether I will ever arrive. I write from the midst of things and I cannot see their order as yet.... I want to run but I can only drag along slowly. You know that I do not take pen in hand with the prior intention of following a system and of marching at random toward an end; I give myself over to the natural flow of ideas, allowing myself to be borne in good faith from one consequence to another.

This is of course the same procedure used by almost all writers who care about style and are not from the outset locked into their ideas—those who consider writing an act of discovery. But in the case of *Democracy in America,* Tocqueville had greater problems than simple composition. The problem of tone, the level of generality required by such a book, whose pretensions to describing and analyzing the significance of the political institutions and social arrangements of a new and largely unknown country, were more than considerable.

As for his *idée mere,* Tocqueville announced it in the first sentence of his introduction to *Democracy in America:* "Among the new things that attracted my attention during my stay in the United States, none struck me more forcefully than the equality of conditions." That single word "equality" set off in his mind a Catherine wheel of related ideas and questions. Liberty, centralization, the place of religion in the foundation of states, the significance of *moeurs* (or customs, beliefs, and social values) and their relation to laws, the role of historical circumstance—what was the influence of equality on them and of them on equality? "As I pursued my study of American society," Tocqueville wrote in his introduction to *Democracy in America*, "I therefore came increasingly to see the equality of conditions as the original fact from which each particular fact seem to derive. It stood constantly before me as the focal point toward which all my observations converged."

Tocqueville never wrote more revealingly for the public than in his introduction to *Democracy in America*. More than once, he strikes the religious note: "This book was written in the grip of a kind of religious terror occasioned in the soul of its author by the sight of this irresistible revolution [of equality].... We can discern indubitable signs of God's will [in this overwhelming rise of equality] even if God Himself remains silent." He calls "the gradual development of the equality of conditions ... a providential fact.... It is universal, durable, and daily proves itself to be beyond the reach of man's powers." A few pages later he writes: "Without morality freedom cannot reign, and without faith there is no morality." He adds: "I would rather doubt my sanity than God's justice." Such comments are in no way perfunctory, the polite obeisance of a man invoking the deity as a matter of good form. The religious question, the role of God in the affairs of men and women, was never for very long out of Tocqueville's mind.

His introduction also makes plain that while the book is about the United States, it is intended quite as much, perhaps more, for a French readership than any other. The experience of democracy was America's, but it was the French who needed to draw the correct lessons from it. For democracy in France, in Tocqueville's view, has thus far been little short of a disaster. "French democracy, hindered in its forward progress or left to cope unaided with its own unruly passions, toppled anything that stood in its way, shaking what it did not destroy." Wherever he looks, Tocqueville finds "nothing to excite greater sorrow and pity than what is taking place before our very eyes. The natural bonds that join opinion to taste and action to belief seem lately to have been broken. The harmony that has been observed throughout [French] history between man's feelings and his ideas has apparently been destroyed, and the laws of moral analogy have seemingly been abolished."

Here Tocqueville is referring to the heavy toll that the French Revolution continued to take, even though it was more than forty years in the past. For Tocqueville the revolution, though chronologically well over before his birth, staggered on with dire consequence throughout his life, or so he continued to feel; the instability, the volatility, the shabbiness of French political life, all were the legacy of the revolution, whose reverberations knew no surcease. "Having destroyed an aristocratic society," he tells his countrymen, "we seem ready to go on living complacently amid the rubble forever."

Although Tocqueville announces that he wishes to study democracy "to find out what we had to hope or fear from it," he never idealizes it or aristocracy. He grants that the new (and, to his mind, inevitable) "democratic society would be less brilliant than an aristocracy but also less plagued by misery." Neither a reactionary nor a progress-monger, he does assert that under democracy the opportunity for greatness in every field—political, military, artistic—will be less; and, for so ambitious a man as he, this is no minor detraction.

Still, Tocqueville thought, one must live in the time appointed, play out the cards dealt one, which to him meant that "the primary duty imposed on the leaders of society today" was "to educate democracy—if possible to revive its beliefs, to purify its mores, to regulate its impulses, to substitute, little by little, knowledge of affairs for inexperience and understanding of true interests for blind instinct, to adapt government to its time and place, to alter it to fit circumstances and time." This was a new world, totally new, and such a world, Tocqueville wrote, "demands a new political science." Not yet thirty, far distant from any semblance of personal power, in many ways the pure type of the intellectual, Tocqueville (can one doubt it?) saw himself as one of those leaders who would educate democracy—specifically, democracy in France—and he would do so by creating the new political science which he himself had called for.

The way Tocqueville would accomplish both was through his book. There remained only to write it properly. Not only had he to honor the immense complexity of his subject but he had to attain the right level of generality in setting it out. When he came to discuss the judicial institutions of the United States, for example, Tocqueville openly reported his fear of not getting things right, noting: "But how can I make the political action of American courts clear without going into detail about their constitution and procedures? And how can I delve in detail into such an intrinsically arid subject without repelling the reader? How can I remain clear without ceasing to be brief?"

Taking the quick breath permitted by a paragraph break, he continues: "I do not flatter myself that I have avoided these various perils. Men of the world will find me tedious; lawyers will think me superficial. But this is a drawback inherent in the subject in general as well as in the more specialized material with which I am about to deal."

By the time he wrote this, Tocqueville had already found his method. This was to be descriptive and analytical and philosophical—all, somehow, simultaneously. To do this, one must be accurate, lucid, penetrating, and wise. Not an easy trick, and thus not, as a method, available to everyone. Young as he was when he wrote the first part of *Democracy in America,* it was already available to Tocqueville. His mastery of this method in good part constitutes his genius.

Consider, briefly, Tocqueville's pages on the election and reelection to office of the president of the United States. After describing the role and responsibilities of the American president, he arrives at the presidential elections. Tocqueville notes the frenzy that they bring on. "As the election draws near, intrigues intensify, and agitation increases and spreads. The citizens divide into several camps, each behind its candidate. A fever grips the entire nation. The election becomes the daily grist of the public papers, the subject of private conversation, the aim of all activity, the object of all thought, the sole interest of the moment." And then it is over, and "ardor dissipates, calm is restored, and the river, having briefly overflowed its banks, returns peacefully to its bed." Sounds like the last American election, does it not, and also doubtless like the next one.

When it comes to the reelection of presidents, Tocqueville turns up the critical wattage. He underscores the advantage that presidents in office seeking reelection have over rivals without the power of the government behind them. He points out that "it is impossible to observe the ordinary course of affairs in the United States without noticing that the desire to be re-elected dominates the thoughts of the president; that the whole policy of his administration is directed toward this end, his every action bent to this purpose; and that, particularly when the crisis looms, his own individual interest supplants the general interest in his mind." At such a time the president seeking reelection "prostrates himself before the majority"; he governs less in the interest of the people than in his own; and the whole exercise "tends to degrade the nation's political morality and to substitute shrewdness for patriotism."

Things get worse. A president who did not have to worry about reelection would have been accountable to the people without being dependent on them. He could steer a smoother course between the majority will and good sense, not having to bend so obviously to the former. This notion of essentially whoring after votes greatly detracts from the dignity of office, in Tocqueville's view, "especially now that political morality has grown lax and men of great character are vanishing from office."

All this was written without Tocqueville's having had direct experience of an American presidential election. Only eleven elections had been held at the time of his visit to the United States; twelve, when he sat down to the composition of his book. How did he come into possession of such accurate knowledge of the spirit of our presidential elections? Some of this knowledge doubtless came from the many people he interviewed while in the United States. Some came from *The Federalist* and other readings. But quite as much, I suspect, came from his own powers of intuition and extrapolation. All this, both description and analysis, remains perfectly valid today.

Tocqueville was especially taken with the level of political education available in the United States. The spread of the franchise (though the vote had not yet been given to women) and universal schooling brought people up a level of political awareness beyond that generally available in Europe. Americans were further educated by serving on juries, by running for office, and above all by forming and belonging to the country's multifarious voluntary associations. (Today in America, in commemoration of Tocqueville's admiration of our voluntary associations, there are nearly 400 chapters of the Tocqueville Society, whose members have contributed $10,000 or more to their local United Fund.)

Considering the American Constitution, with its subtle blurring of a federation and a nation, Tocqueville writes: "The human mind invents things more readily than words. That is why so many improper terms and inadequate expressions are in use." What was invented by the American framers of the Constitution is a new theory, and indeed a new form, of government: "one," Tocqueville writes, "that was neither precisely national nor precisely federal. To date, that is as far as anyone has gone; the new word that ought to express this new thing does not yet exist." Nor, one might add, does it exist today. That this French visitor, sitting down to write about it after a hectic nine-month visit, himself not yet thirty years old, understood so perfectly what the Americans had invented, is a further sign of Tocqueville's brilliance.

Tocqueville put in a little less than a year completing what would be published as the first volume of *Democracy in America*. A very strenuous, intellectually feverish year it was. As he wrote, he sent around portions of his manuscript to his father, to Beaumont, to his brothers, to Louis de Kergorlay and Eugène Stoffels and other friends, for their corrections and criticisms. He took their responses seriously, and on the basis of these responses, made serious alterations in the final draft of his book.

"My life is regulated like that of a monk," Tocqueville wrote to Kergorlay about his activities during that year. "From morning to night my existence is completely intellectual, and at night I go to Marie's house [Marie, or Mary, Mottley, the Englishwoman whom he eventually married].... The next day I begin again, and so on with a surprising regularity, because my books and Marie form exactly my entire existence since my return from England. It is difficult for me to live for others and others for me."

Did Tocqueville know that he was writing a masterpiece? Given his often faltering self-confidence, my guess is, probably not. The world, however, would soon assure him that this was precisely what, during those long days scribbling away in the attic on the rue de Verneuil, he had been doing.

Chapter Five

THE BOOK, published in January 1835, was a smashing success, critical and commercial. This came as a surprise to its publisher, who had run off a first edition of 500 copies. No one knows the number of copies sold over the next four years, though it went through seven printings. English and German translations soon appeared. In a disputatious and politically motivated French press, critics all agreed on the talent, depth of analysis, and wisdom displayed by its author. Sainte-Beuve said of *Democracy in America* that "one would have to look far and wide among us to find another book of science and political observation that would arouse and satisfy the attention of thoughtful minds to this extent." Tocqueville's intellectual rocket had hit its target; the first half of his book on the new democracy of America—a second half was promised—was regarded as a masterpiece, nothing less.

Alexis de Tocqueville had arrived. He was suddenly a young man worth knowing. He was invited, through his cousin

Chateaubriand, to the famous salon of Madame de Récamier. Political connections followed hard upon social ones. Tocqueville became the friend and protégé of Pierre-Paul Royer-Collard, a key figure in the Chamber of Deputies during the years of the Bourbon restoration. The Académie Française awarded *Democracy in America* a Montyon Prize, this time for 12,000 francs. Its author was elected to the Academy of Moral and Political Sciences; election to the Académie Française would come later, in 1841. While all the attention must have been immensely satisfying, the young author, as we shall see, yearned more for political than intellectual distinction.

Tocqueville, meanwhile, married. His marriage to Mary Mottley, an Englishwoman about nine years older than he (her exact age is not known), not particularly attractive, and with neither social standing nor a large fortune, has been something of a puzzle to Tocqueville's biographers. The details of both the courtship and the marriage remain muzzy, even after the expert researches of the estimable M. Jardin and others.

Tocqueville and Marie (as he called her) apparently met in 1828 or 1829, when Tocqueville was a magistrate in Versailles, where was she living with an aunt, one Mrs. Belam, the widow of a pharmacist in Portsmouth, who had raised her. Miss Mottley had brothers in the British navy. She was middle-class English, not a bad thing to be unless your suitor happens to come from a family of French aristocrats. Drawings show Mary Mottley to be a woman of refined features, though with a long upper lip covering what Antoine Redier, a biographer of Tocqueville's who was not partial to her, described as "yellow" teeth. He also described her as having "severe eyes." Her health was delicate, like her husband's, and she suffered from rheumatism, erysipelas, and other afflictions. "Mme. de Tocqueville was somewhat unwell in Berne" is a sentence of a kind that shows up often in her husband's correspondence, with only the place-names changing. In *The Making of Democracy in America*, James T. Schleifer writes of the couple that "it almost seemed that when one wasn't ill, the other was." Tocqueville, we know from Jardin, suffered from migraines, pleurisy, serious attacks of neuralgia, difficult digestion, stomach cramps, and—the illness that is believed to have killed him—pulmonary tuberculosis.

Tocqueville balked at the idea of an arranged marriage to someone of his own class. That suggests rebellion, yet he was most patient in riding out his family's and friends' objections before marrying Miss Mottley; there was a gap of six or seven years between their meeting and their marriage in 1835. Even her becoming a serious Catholic (and, it was said, sometimes rather an intolerant one) did little to improve her position with her husband's family. For most of the marriage, she kept her distance from her in-laws. Lord Acton recalls a conversation in which the subject of marrying beneath one's station arose, at which point Tocqueville, grasping his wife's hand, remarked, "I, too, married beneath me, and by God it was worth it."

Letters from Tocqueville to his wife attest to his gratitude for her support and understanding of his complex and often difficult temperament. A tightly wound man of volatile nature, Tocqueville wrote to Louis de Kergorlay about Marie's calming effect on him: "She makes me tolerant of many men and actions that I would have condemned without remission several years ago." When his nephew Hubert was contemplating marriage, Tocqueville wrote him: "There is nothing solid and truly sweet in this world but domestic happiness and intimacy with a wife who knows how to understand you, to help you, if need be to support you in the difficulties of life. I have felt that too much from my own experience not to be convinced of it. At bottom, it is only in a father or in a wife that true and continual sympathy can be found."

Tocqueville wrote to Kergorlay that not having a child was the only "sweet emotion" he has not known, adding: "So, that is the sole plank of safety I see in the future and if by misfortune, M. should not become a mother, I would entirely despair of my existence." But they had no children; she was forty when they married and he less than robust. Their parental emotions were placed instead in a series of pug dogs.

A wise man once said that neither marriage nor bachelorhood was a fit solution. (Let us leave aside for now what, precisely, is the problem.) Certainly neither was a solution for a man as high-strung and imaginative as Tocqueville. His biographers tell a story about his wife's habit of eating so slowly that one day, unable to abide it any longer, he rose from his chair, took her plate of pâté, and dashed it to the floor. (She, without a change of expression, is said insouciantly to have ordered another.) He complained to Beaumont of his wife's lack of reason, for "her reason serves her only up to a point, beyond which she lapses into the unreasonable." He groused a good deal about the noise and confusion brought about by the work-men his wife hired to refurbish the château in Normandy he had inherited on his mother's death—they lived summer and fall in Normandy, winter and spring in Paris—though he was subsequently pleased by the comfort her alterations had made in it. They spoke English when alone together. She was not an uncultivated person; she spoke German, for example, while her husband did not. When she appears in the journals of Tocque-ville's English friend, the political economist Nassau Senior, Marie de Tocqueville always speaks sensibly and knowledge-ably. In *Recollections,* his memoir of the revolution of 1848, Tocqueville more than once remarks on the steadfastness of his wife during a time of tumult: "I could count at home on the support of a devoted wife of penetrating insight and staunch spirit, whose naturally lofty soul would be ready to face any situation and triumph over any setback."

And yet, late in his life, Tocqueville choose to write to Sophie Swetchine about his deepest sadness, reporting that he felt "vague restlessness and an incoherent agitation of desires that have always been a chronic malady with me." He goes on to say that he should by all rights be happy, "the tranquil enjoy-ment of the present good being sufficient for most men," and he perhaps above most men, given his wife, who has established serenity in his home. Yet this tranquillity, this serenity, "soon escapes me and abandons me to this turmoil that is without cause or effect, which often makes my soul turn a wheel that has fallen out of gear." Hugh Brogan notes that Tocqueville's wife "was mother, lover, nurse, and companion to him." Still, writing to Kergorlay on September 27, 1843, Tocqueville confesses that his strong sexual nature has led him into several infidelities, and left him with much guilt and nowhere to relieve it. He went to church each Sunday with Marie, yet never, according to M. Jardin, revealed his religious skepticism to her.

Tocqueville, one must conclude, was not intended to be happy. Despite all his gifts and natural advantages, his ambition would always override and cripple his happiness. International literary celebrity, even at the level on which he achieved it, would never be sufficient; he craved a life of action, political action. Such a life would allow him, or so he thought before entering it, not only to put his political ideas to work but to pursue his destiny.

Until the July Revolution of the summer of 1830, resulting in the abdication of Charles X and the accession of Louis-Philippe to power, Tocqueville would have had the prospect of an active political life forestalled by law. Before the July Revolution, one had to be forty to serve in the Chamber of Deputies; the July Revolution lowered the age to thirty, which meant that by 1835, Tocqueville qualified, though he held back from running for election until 1837.

He could have run out of four possible voting districts. M. Jardin recounts in more detail than is required here how he eventually settled on the fourth, that of the Valognes *arrondissement,* in Normandy, ten miles from the château and estate he had inherited. The opposing candidate and the current deputy, a certain Comte Jules-Polydor Le Marois, son of a former aide-de-camp to Napoleon, had been accused, apparently quite rightly, of corruption.

Checked Out Items 8/31/2016 19:20
XXXXXXXXXX2642

Item Title	Due Date
31132009503414	9/21/2015
Alexis de Tocqueville : democracy's guide	

Amount Outstanding: $3.50

708 383 8200
log in learn more oppl.org

OAK PARK PUBLIC LIBRARY

oppl.org

Checked Out Items 8/31/2015 19:20

XXXXXXXXXXXX2642

Item Title	Due Date
31132009903414	9/21/2015
Alexis de Tocqueville : democracy's guide	

Amount Outstanding: $3.50

708.383.8200

log in, learn more: oppl.org

Alexis de Tocqueville, high theoretician of democracy, now has his rather refined nose rubbed into the grubbiness of electoral politics. Le Marois had lots of money, which he didn't mind spending on entertaining electors at banquets, plying them with wine at taverns, and finding ways of being chummy with them in the best glad-handing tradition of ward politics. Le Marois was also connected, through family, with the sub-prefect in charge of collecting taxes—a position that allowed him to provide electors with slower, more convenient ways of paying their taxes. Tocqueville's cousin Comte Louis-Mathieu Mole, the ranking minister of the current government, offered his help in the election. Too proud to avail himself of the offer, Tocqueville informed Mole that he didn't wish to go into the Chamber of Deputies owing any political debts.

Le Marois concentrated his fire on agricultural issues of prime interest to the voters in the district: animal husbandry policy and such. Taking the high road, Tocqueville promised protection of liberty and the prevention of destabilizing revolution, claiming to be neither for absolute rule nor for a republic—all politically quite sound but not exactly gut issues at the level of local politics. In anonymous pamphlets, Le Marois's forces depicted Tocqueville as a snobbish aristocrat. ("No more noblemen" was the slogan of the anti-Tocqueville crowd.) One of Tocqueville's two replies to these pamphlets was never delivered by the local postal chief, also thought to be Le Marois's man. And yet for all this Tocqueville lost in a second-round election by only twenty-seven votes, 247 to 220.

When the Chamber of Deputies was dissolved in 1839,

Tocqueville was ready for another run. Le Marois's position had further weakened; corruption charges against him were still in the air. Tocqueville had been sedulously cultivating the voters of Valognes, and more local support had rallied around him. To the charge that he was a coldly distant aristocrat, he responded by saying, with *Democracy in America* as evidence, that "in all of France and, I daresay, in all of Europe, there is not one man who has demonstrated more publicly that the old aristocracy is dead." In another letter to the electors, he carved out his position: he was "attached to certain principles, but I am not tied to a party. I am even more firmly independent where the government is concerned; I am not a government candidate and I do not in the least want to be one." He was elected by a first-round vote of 318 to 240. When his victory was announced, the local farmers walked him to his château, from the window of which Tocqueville declared: "I go, my heart filled with the memory of my friends, but, as of this day, I wish to say that I have forgot all the names of my honorable opponents."

Tocqueville had been working on the second part of *Democracy in America,* but the notion of being in the whirl of active politics in Paris was much more seductive to him. "Do not believe that I have a blind enthusiasm, or indeed any kind of enthusiasm for the intellectual life," he wrote to Kergorlay. "I have always placed the life of action above everything else." He went on to say that he recognized that writing could itself be a powerful mode of action. In later years, in conversation with Nassau Senior, looking back on his brief tenure as foreign secretary under the Second Republic, Tocqueville said: "What I regret of my ministerial functions is the labor and absorption. I delighted in not knowing a moment of the day to myself. I am naturally, perhaps, melancholy, and when it has nothing else to do, my mind preys upon itself."

What a stir his presence in the Chamber of Deputies must have caused in Tocqueville! After such long thinking and writing about politics, he was now at last *in* politics, *doing* politics, himself an actual politician. He was too alert not to have grasped in careful detail the various political alignments in the Chamber of Deputies. What came more and more to impress him—depress him, more precisely—was how many of his fellow deputies were chiefly in business for themselves. This young man, with his powerful engine of cerebration, did not miss much, and the squalor of the Chamber of Deputies, everyone rushing about cutting his own deals, gave him reasons for demoralization.

In the earlier lost election, the compte de Mole, after having his offer of help refused, instructed Tocqueville on the crucial point that there was a difference between independence and isolation. Now a member of the Chamber of Deputies, Tocqueville was in danger of isolating himself by attempting to remain free of party connections. At that time, in the chamber itself, one sat according to one's politics— put one's bottom, so to say, where one's political views were. Tocqueville found a seat left of center, between the republican and dynastic left; he was fundamentally liberal, but for now continued to believe (though not very ardently) in monarchy while hoping that a steady and tranquil shift to democracy could be achieved. M. Jardin neatly sets out the particularities of Tocqueville's political positions: "the separation of Church and State, reform of the suffrage laws [by extending them to a larger percentage of the population], revision of the tax structure to the advantage of the workers, the freedom of local schools to choose their own curricula, the abolition of slavery [in Algeria and the French colonies], a broad investigation of poverty for the purpose of eliminating it through the formation of associations, etc."

Active politics was a minefield—some might say a dog run—through which Tocqueville walked most gingerly. He was, as the political scientist Sheldon Wolin nicely put it, "a nonconformist without being a rebel." Tocqueville later wrote that he entered the Chamber of Deputies as "a new man with a free spirit and an ardent and sincere love of representative government and of the dignity of the country." Such a spirit did not easily find suitable companions in the year 1839. The poet Alphonse de Lamartine was a fellow deputy many of whose views Tocqueville shared, but he worried about being swept up by the strong character of Lamartine, clearly a coming man. Louis Thiers and François Guizot, the dominating figures during Tocqueville's years in the Chamber, were both politically repugnant to him. He claimed Thiers had adroitness but no principles, while everyone else had "neither adroitness nor principles." Guizot, from whose lectures he had once learned so much, now seemed to him another operator-politician. So talented in their different ways, these two men, owing to their want of political vision, were less great than they should have been; in their separate careers, they set the seal of mediocrity on the period they dominated.

Tocqueville's independence, and his high standard of political judgment, brought him little satisfaction. Sixty new deputies were elected when he was, and he had hopes that many of them would join him in something resembling an antiparty party working outside the old arrangements of self-interest and standard alignments. Later in his tenure in the Chamber of Deputies, he wrote to a fellow deputy that he longed for "an association of a few men of talent and good heart who would not involve themselves in intrigue ... but work at what there was to be done for its own sake." Even if this could be brought off, he, alas, wasn't the man to do it: his manner was too coolly—not to say coldly—aloof, whereas cozening familiarity was needed to form strong political groups. "To be a success in public," said his cousin Chateaubriand, "it is not a question of acquiring qualities but of losing them."

So much about the active political life was alien to Tocqueville's nature. He soon learned, as he put it in his *Recollections*, his memoir of his years in active politics, that he "completely lacked the art of holding men together and leading them as a body. It was only in tête-à-tête that I show any dexterity, whereas in a crowd I am constrained and dumb." He also lacked "intense sociability" and had no taste, either, for the "constant repetition" that is part of political argument. His integrity everywhere got in the way. His devotion to what he took to be the truth was such that, "once I had found it, I do not want to risk it in the hazard of an argument; I feel it is like a light that might be put out by waving it to and fro." In short, he "was not slow to discover that I lacked the qualities needed to play the brilliant role of which I dreamed; both my good qualities and my defects proved obstacles."

No one was less hail-fellow or less easily well met; he lacked the gift of making himself quickly liked. His physical frailty; his myopia; even the pallor of his skin, which some took to be a sign of his spoiling ambition; his ironic manner ("One can see that his words give more than one meaning," a man noted on first meeting him)—all worked against him.

Tocqueville had no hope of distinguishing himself in the Chamber of Deputies through oratorical talent, and eloquence was of course much more highly valued there than intellectual penetration. His problem with public speaking went back to his days as a young magistrate in Versailles, whence, in 1827, he wrote to Louis de Kergorlay: "I am finding it difficult to become used to speaking in public; I grope for my words and I pay too much attention to my ideas. All about me I see people who reason badly and who speak well; that continually throws me into despair. It seems to me that I am above them, but whenever I make an appearance, I feel beneath them."

Potent extemporaneous speech would never be his strength; he had a thin voice and little in the way of personal presence. He was too thoughtful, too intent on precision, to be effective on his feet. That he wrote as well as he did only worked against him. In a talk he gave to the Academy of Political and Moral Sciences in 1853, he said: "The art of writing does, in fact, give to those who have long practiced it habits of mind unfavorable to the conduct of affairs. It makes them subject to the logic of ideas, where the mob obeys only that of its passions. It gives a taste for what is delicate, fine, ingenious, and original, where the veriest commonplaces rule the world." In the second volume of *Democracy in America,* with perhaps himself in mind, Tocqueville wrote that "to remain silent is the most useful service that a mediocre speaker can render to the public good."

Tocqueville's friend Royer-Collard, the moderate royalist deputy who through his high intelligence, philosophical temperament, and good sense managed to keep his dignity and the regard of all members of the Chamber of Deputies during an especially squalid period in French politics, had earlier warned him against seeking election to the Chamber of Deputies, saying that he was entering active political life at a most unstable time and that, without the gift of oratory, was doing so at a real disadvantage. More than forty years older than Tocqueville, Royer-Collard served as his adviser and, often, confessor during Tocqueville's early years in the Chamber. (Royer-Collard died in 1843.)

Yet in his home district of Valognes, where he carefully cultivated the electors, Tocqueville was much admired. He was thrice made president of the departmental, or local, council. On the council he allowed his large-gauge mind to occupy itself on smaller-gauge matters. He traveled around, informing local officials and landowners about the politics of Paris. M. Jardin recounts a charming anecdote about how, on the day of an election, one of the electors remarked that Tocqueville looked tired, and wondered why, since they had all carried him to the election in their pocket—a reference to the already filled-out ballots on which they had registered their votes in his favor.

Identifying and locking in Tocqueville's political position has become an unending game that is finally a mug's game, or one that cannot be won. Was he a man of the left or the right, a liberal or a conservative, a conservative-liberal or a liberal-conservative, a sentimental aristocrat or a grudging democrat? The truth seems to be that he was all these things, sometimes separately and sometimes nearly simultaneously—all these things and more. He feared revolution (with good historical cause) and admired order; he despised demagoguery; he was no friend to the masses, at least taken in the bulky abstract way the term is generally used, yet he understood completely the emotional charge that the feeling of injustice brings. He was vehemently against slavery, yet for colonialism. Nothing about Tocqueville's politics was simple.

These politics were conditioned in good part by historical circumstances. In a letter of March 22, 1837, to Henry Reeve, his friend and English translator, Tocqueville wrote: "Democratic or aristocratic prejudices are alternatively attributed to me; I would perhaps have had one or the other had I been born in another century and country. But accident of birth has left me free to defend both.... The aristocracy was already dead when I was born, and democracy was still not in being. My instincts could not therefore be drawn blindly toward either one or the other. I was born in a country that for forty years tried a little of everything without concentrating on anything, and I was not therefore an easy prey to political illusions. Being myself of the old aristocracy of my country, I felt no natural hatred or envy against it; and as this aristocracy had been destroyed I had no more natural love for it, since we are strong partisans only of the living.... In a word, I was so much in equilibrium between the past and future that I did not feel naturally and instinctively drawn toward either one or the other, and had no difficulty in looking dispassionately at the two sides."

But in politics a man without clear positions is, as M. Mole predicted, sooner rather than later, alone. And so Tocqueville found himself in the Chamber of Deputies. He discovered himself sympathizing with the right yet lining up more often than not with the left, though usually, on either side, in opposition to the government. He was appointed *rapporteur*, or the man designated to write up findings, on two important committees: those on slavery and on the prison system, subjects on which his visit to the United States had given him something of the standing of an expert. Early in his term he spoke before the Chamber of Deputies on foreign policy in the Middle East, though not to much effect. He hedged a bit on the question of slavery in Algeria, then a French colony, holding that slavery should be eliminated in stages instead of coming out for full and immediate abolition. He interested himself in foreign policy. He defended French independence and, whenever possible, plumped for national grandeur. He spoke in the debate over the liberty of provincial teaching, which he didn't wish to see dominated by the centralized universities of Paris. He came to the defense of localized governing bodies, fearing as always that too much centralization of government was a path to despotism. By 1846, reelected yet again as a deputy, Tocqueville, in M. Jardin's words, had acquired "a certain weight in the political world and definitely cut an original figure." Yet, as Seymour Drescher has written, Tocqueville's "nine years in the Chamber of Deputies were passed in helpless frustration. He failed to become a real leader in the Chamber. All his major programs or recommendations were defeated or stymied." He must have looked upon the Chamber of Deputies as an intellectual, if not perhaps also a moral, slum.

Defeat and frustration are the major notes in Tocqueville's letters to Royer-Collard during this period. He begins, in a letter of 1840, by telling the older man how difficult it is to talk with the voters in his district, many of whom didn't know who was currently prime minister. "Do you believe, Monsieur, you who have seen so much and reflected so much, and probed so deeply into human nature, do you believe that the political world will long remain as destitute of true passions as it is at this moment and that it will be for a long time as far out of style as it is now to bring to it, as an element of success, a sincere taste for working for the general good?" In a somewhat self-congratulatory manner, he goes on to ask, "Do you believe, Monsieur, that a time may come in which a love of the public good, as disinterested as our poor human nature permits, can render some service and finally put integrity in a place of honor? I love the good, but I also love the success that it brings." The honesty of the second half of that sentence saves Tocqueville from being a perfect political prig, trumpeting his own virtue.

A year later, things haven't improved. Tocqueville was learning that he really had little vocation for active politics. He reports to Royer-Collard his distaste for both Thiers and Guizot, and yet allows that, outside their spheres of influence, nothing can get done. "I compare myself to a wheel that goes around very quickly, but which, having missed its gear, does nothing and is useful for nothing." He adds that he "feels an almost invincible repugnance to associating myself in a permanent manner with any of the political men of our times and, among all the parties that divide our country, I do not see a single one to which I would want to be tied." All that is left to him, he feels, is to express himself as well as he can on the events and laws of the day, but without any hope of usefully altering either, and to keep such moral force as he has intact by not squandering it for petty advantage. "Reason," he complains, "has always been for me like a cage that keeps me from acting, but not from gnashing my teeth behind the bars."

As for Royer-Collard's view of Tocqueville, M. Jardin quotes a letter from Royer-Collard to the duchesse de Dino in which he writes that the young Tocqueville "has a fund of honesty that is not enough for him, that he spends imprudently, but of which something will always be left: I fear that because of his impatience to arrive, he will stray into impracticable paths, trying to reconcile what is irreconcilable." The wise Royer-Collard also recognized that Tocqueville was aflame with ambition and impatient to land in a position of eminence.

In his *Recollections* Tocqueville looked back on his days in the Chamber of Deputies under the monarchy of King Louis-

Philippe. He recalled it as a time when the middle class "had settled into every [government] office, prodigiously increased the number of offices, and made a habit of living off the public Treasury almost as much as from its own industry." Louis-Philippe had set all this in motion: "he was the accident that made the illness fatal." He compared the government to a "trading company," with everyone out for his own interests.

As for his fellow deputies, Tocqueville wrote: "I spent ten years of my life in the company of truly great minds who were in a constant state of agitation without every really becoming heated, and who expended all their perspicacity in the vain search for subjects on which they could seriously disagree." Louis-Philippe's ideas so dominated all proceedings in the Chamber of Deputies that the differences between the parties were reduced to "slight nuances" and the contest among them to a "quarrel over words." Legitimists, Socialists, Catholics, Republicans, Patriots, Liberals, and the *tiers parti*—all specialized in disagreeing among themselves and had no solution to the problem of moving Louis-Philippe into making useful changes. The deputies "were bored with listening to one another, and, what was worse, the whole nation was bored with hearing them."

After the defeat of his first election attempt, Tocqueville received a letter of consolation from Royer-Collard, in which the older man noted that the younger was "guided by Providence," and that "the life of a deputy today is a trivial one if not a stupefying one for most of the deputies. You cannot seek fame in it; you must bring fame to it. Finish your book then; that will be a providential sign." Royer-Collard, once again, was to prove correct. Much later, in 1852, retired from active politics, Tocqueville wrote to his father that he had "never desired power, only reputation." But this was written at time when for him power was no longer a serious possibility. The truth was that he longed ardently for both power and reputation.

Chapter Six

IN THE INTRODUCTION to *Democracy in America*, Tocqueville provided a little advertisement for a second part of the work—a part not to be written by him. He mentioned that he did originally plan to write this second part, one describing "the influence of equality of conditions and democratic government on civil society in America: on habits, ideas, and mores." But his ardor for the project had begun to wane, and, besides, he averred, "soon another author will set the principal traits of American character before the reader. By concealing the gravity of his portrait beneath a light veil, he will adorn truth with greater charm than I am capable of." This Salome of analysis was of course to have been Gustave de Beaumont.

The Tocqueville-Beaumont partnership is perhaps without an analogue in intellectual history. Beaumont had become a member of the Chamber of Deputies the same year as Tocqueville (1839), and for the most part—with one small glitch, when they took up different positions—they worked there as a team in opposition to the government. They traveled to England and Ireland together; they married in the same year; they worked on parallel projects. Beaumont even served as Tocqueville's nurse when Tocqueville became ill in the United States and on another occasion when they were together in Algeria.

Their intellectual partnership was nearly complete. Beaumont had in part handled the subject adumbrated in Tocqueville's introduction to the first volume of *Democracy in America*—the "habits, ideas, and mores" of the Americans—in his novel *Marie*. But it was now decided that Tocqueville would work up this material in his own, rather more complex fashion. How it came about that Tocqueville would after all go it alone on the second volume of *Democracy in America* is not known with any precision.

The two men had worked out a division of labor: this at any rate is what Seymour Drescher suggests, in a splendid appendix he wrote to a book he edited, *Tocqueville and Beaumont on Social Reform*. Under this division, Beaumont would take up the sympathetic treatments of such underdogs as Negro slaves, American Indians, and the Irish, while Tocqueville would describe and analyze the more central streams of power. Beaumont would thus write about Ireland (as he did in *L'Irlande* in 1838) and England, leaving America and pre- and postrevolutionary France to Tocqueville. Tocqueville also wrote about England, but he published none of these writings during his lifetime.

In attempting to do justice to Beaumont, Drescher emphasizes that the two men talked over everything. Tocqueville, we know, sent his manuscripts to Beaumont (among others) for criticism and correction, and so one cannot always be certain what precisely in both volumes of *Democracy in America* belongs to Beaumont and what to Tocqueville. What isn't in doubt is that of the two men, Tocqueville had much the greater analytical power; his was the mind that made the striking connections, generating ideas from facts, generalizations from analysis. Tocqueville's work was no doubt made much better owing to the aid of Beaumont, but Beaumont, with all the help in the world from Tocqueville, is unlikely to have produced a book as richly complex as *Democracy in America*.

During the composition of the second volume, Tocqueville often wrote to the friends he had made in the United States, asking them to fill him in on material he himself hadn't been able to gather during his brief visit. He continued to read everything pertinent to his project that he could obtain: *The Federalist*, James Kent's *Commentaries on American Law,* Joseph Story's *Commentaries on the Constitution of the United States,* and a vast deal more. He was attempting to complete the second volume of his book just as his active political career was getting under way. "I must at all costs finish this book," he wrote to Beaumont. "It and I have a duel to the death—and I must kill it or it must kill me."

Despite the magisterial tone of the completed book, Tocqueville knew how tentative his procedure in this book was: his method of analysis leading to general ideas. He knew the limitations of even good ideas to capture the richness of reality. God, he wrote in an early chapter, "has no need of general ideas," but the human mind cannot endure without them. "General ideas attest not to the strength of the human intellect but rather to its insufficiency.... General ideas are admirable in one respect [only], namely, that they allow the human mind to make rapid judgments about a great many things at once, but the notions they provide are always incomplete, and what they gain in breadth they lose in exactitude." This distrust for general ideas marks Tocqueville as a man of essentially literary sensibility, for whom the important truths are to be found either in particular cases or above the level of ideas in the realm of the truths of the human heart.

That passage from *Democracy in America* is part of Tocqueville's apologia for his own procedure of hit-and-run ideas in his study of democracy. Although the profligacy of ideas in the book all issue out of the *idée mère* of the irresistible rise of equality in the world of Tocqueville's time, the fundamental movement from which everything else in the book derives, these ideas, in his recounting of them, do pass with blazing quickness. What amazes is the cogency of so many of them and the intellectual fecundity of the man who generated them.

Other Tocquevillian generalizations make one wonder about their autobiographical content. In his chapter "How Equality of Conditions Helps to Maintain Good Morals in America," Tocqueville, taking up the Americans' insistence on free choice in marriage, writes: "No one should be surprised, therefore, that if a man in an aristocratic society makes so bold as to rely solely on his own private opinion and taste when choosing a mate, moral disorder and misery may soon overtake his household." Reading this, one hears the crash of that plate of pâté *chez* Tocqueville and recalls Tocqueville's confession of infidelities.

Everywhere aphoristic sentences strike the gong of compelling truth. "No one can work harder at being happier than Americans do," writes Tocqueville, and one immediately thinks of our high per capita participation in psychotherapy. "Habitual inattention must be regarded as the greatest defect of the American mind," he writes, and one thinks of the nation of ADD children in our midst and their scarcely more concentrated parents. "Variety," he notes, "is vanishing from the human species," and one thinks of the indigenes on view around the world wearing NBA jerseys and Nike gym shoes.

Democracy in America is a great splendid jumble; its argument is more easily made out than its organization, though the nature of that argument has been the subject of further arguments since the time of its publication. The book is arranged topically, yet critics have wondered why many significant topics seem to have been left out or underemphasized: the rise of such technological advances as railroads in the United States, for one; and American education, for another. Tocqueville himself doubtless thought about this, too, only finally to decide that in such a work one must pick and choose.

The point to keep in mind is that *Democracy in America* is only secondarily about America. The accent in the title needs to be placed on its first word, "democracy," which is the book's true subject, the new republic of the United States constituting a laboratory experiment and illustration of how democracy operates under quite fortunate circumstances. "I confess that in America," Tocqueville wrote, "I saw more than America; I sought the image of democracy itself, with its inclinations, its character, its prejudices, and its passions in order to learn what we have to fear or to hope from its progress."

In the first and in the final analysis, he was less concerned about the fate of democracy across the ocean in the United States than he was about its consequences at home in France. "I did not write one page of [*Democracy in America*] without thinking of her [France] and without having her, so to speak, before my eyes," Tocqueville wrote to a friend in 1847. When one gets well into the second volume, the American aspect of the subject begins more and more to fade. As James Bryce, the English diplomat whose own book, *The American Common- wealth* (1888), is sometimes thought to rival Tocqueville's, put it, "Some [of Tocqueville's] judgments were true of America but not of democracy in general, while others were true of de- mocracy in general but not true of America." M. Jardin adds: "If we tally up the amount of space that facts about America take up in the second [volume of] *Democracy* as a whole, we see that they amount to only about twenty percent of the pages in the first three parts and only two percent in the fourth."

Democracy in America is a hortatory book, a work of advice, warning, and fearful concern. At its center is the inarguable fact of democracy's having arrived, not only in the United States, which has never known anything else, but all over Europe, and, owing to the French Revolution, with a special bolt of lightning and a thunderclap in France. "This entire book," Tocqueville writes in his introduction, "was written in the grip of a kind of religious terror occasioned in the soul of the author by the sight of this irresistible revolution [in the name of equality], which for centuries now has survived every obstacle and continues to advance amid the ruins it has created."

The fateful question is what shape democracy will take in the years ahead. Three main paths are possible: one into anarchy, which Tocqueville seems not much to fear as likely; a second into a tyranny of quiescence ("the tyranny of the majority," or, as Tocqueville sometimes calls it, "democratic despotism"), leading to an undramatic but quite real servitude and unending dreariness of living only for material comforts and out of low self-interest, which he does much fear; and the third path, that of measured progress, on which suffering is less, happiness more widespread, and grandeur much diminished—perhaps the best for which he or anyone else can hope. A question hovers over the entire work: do contemporary societies, especially the French, have the good sense to choose the right path?

A few main themes are at play in *Democracy in America*. "Democracy" itself, of course, is central, though, as many commentators have noted, Tocqueville often used this key term very loosely, sometimes to denote a form of government with a widened suffrage, sometimes to describe a spirit or ethos, sometimes synonymously with equality. His most prevalent sense of democracy, though, was to mean increasing equality of conditions. "Centralization" is another key item, for in Tocqueville's new political science the stronger the centralizing element of a given society, the greater its danger of forfeiting liberty. Tocqueville believed that all governments naturally tended toward centralizing their functions, thus reinforcing their power through ever greater control.

"Liberty," for Tocqueville, is at the very heart of the matter—it is all and everything. Centralization is ever to be feared, for it not only places power in the hands of fewer and fewer people but divests people of the right and then the very ability to manage their own affairs, rendering them vulnerable to tyranny, revolution, or both. "The most important care of good government," Tocqueville wrote in one of his notebooks, "should be to get people used little by little to managing without it"—without government itself, that is. Between the writing of Volume 1 and Volume 2 of *Democracy in America,* Tocqueville wrote to John Stuart Mill, "I love liberty by taste, equality by instinct and reason. These two passions, which so many pretend to have, I am convinced that I really feel in myself, and that I am prepared to make great sacrifices for them." Many have come to doubt that he loved equality at all; they hold that he merely recognized it as a hard fact of political life. His friend Nassau Senior reported Tocqueville as saying to him that "the great misfortune of France is the preference of *égalité* to *liberté*." He described equality during the same conversation as "generally the wish that no one should be better off than oneself," adding that "*égalité* is an expression of envy." As for his love of liberty, he wrote to Mill that he believed liberty "to be useful and necessary, and I work toward it resolutely, without hesitation ... and I hope, without weakness."

The tension in *Democracy in America* derives from Tocqueville's true belief in the inevitability and indeed in the need for equality and his lingering admiration for aristocracy at its best. He once described himself as a democrat of necessity but an aristocrat at heart; and in his private life, whether at his château in Normandy or in Paris, he lived in the manner of an aristocrat—some have suggested in the style of a lordly English landowner.

For Tocqueville democracy was necessary and even morally appropriate, yet he felt that even in its utopian version a purely democratic society would be a rather tepid affair. "Such a society [an orderly, balanced democracy] would be less brilliant than an aristocracy but also less plagued by misery. Pleasures would be less extreme, prosperity more general. Knowledge would be less exalted but ignorance more rare. Feelings would be less passionate and habits milder. There would be more vice and fewer crimes.... In the absence of enthusiasm and ardent belief, citizens could nevertheless be summoned to make great sacrifices by appealing to their reason and experience. All men being equally weak, each would feel equally in need of his fellow man's support and, knowing that cooperation was the condition of that support, would readily see that his private interest was subsumed in the general interest.... The nation taken as a whole would be less brilliant, less glorious, and perhaps less powerful, but the majority of citizens would be better off. People would prefer peace to war, not out of despair of living better but out of appreciation of living well."

Many things about democracy Tocqueville endorsed fully.

He thought family relations were more relaxed and intimate under democracy than under aristocracy, and he approved of this. He thought women more independent and admirable (if less playfully attractive) under democracy. He thought democracy, by making its citizens more alike, also made them more sympathetic, so that they could not view the deaths of large or even small numbers of people with equanimity the way aristocrats seemed able to do.

Yet as endorsements go, Tocqueville's endorsement of democracy is somehow in the end less than ebullient. He found democracy much more impressive in the United States than in France, where, in the still-rippling wake of the French revolution, he saw everything in a state of disarray and diminution. "Everyone senses that something is wrong, but no one has the courage or energy necessary to set it right." Looking toward France, Tocqueville asks: "Has man always confronted, as he does today, a world in which nothing makes sense? In which virtue is without genius and genius without honor? In which the love of order is indistinguishable from the lust of tyrants? In which the sacred cult of liberty is confounded with contempt for the law? In which conscience casts but an ambiguous light on the actions of men? In which nothing any longer seems forbidden or allowed, honest or shameful, true or false?"

Alexis de Tocqueville was a man resigned. The democracy in which he would spend all his life was of limited promise and filled with peril. Yet it was also irresistible. Providence, as he said in his introduction to the first volume of *Democracy in America,* had ordained it. His great project was to show the perils of thoughtless democracy and its most beneficent possibilities.

The limitations Tocqueville saw inherent in democracy chilled him—primarily, in the case of America, the ubiquitous limitations on man's greatness. In a letter of 1831 to his friend Madame de Grancey, he wrote: "In the United States people have neither wars, nor plagues, nor literature, nor eloquence, nor fine arts, few great crimes, nothing of what rouses Europe's attention: here people enjoy the most pallid happiness that one can imagine." (This passage is reminiscent of Henry James, in his book on Hawthorne, describing how little Hawthorne had to work with in American society, which was cause enough for James himself to abandon his native country for Europe.)

The inability of Americans to take what Tocqueville called "the grand view of things" was precisely the kind of diminution that troubled him about life in America and in democracy. "The desire to rise apparently gnaws at every American, yet almost no one seems to nurse vast hopes or to aim very high. All are persistent in their desire to acquire property, reputation, and power," yet, though ambition is "ardent and constant ... people usually spend their lives ardently coveting the petty things they see as being within their reach."

America was the land of the self-made man, and the problem with being self-made is that it takes a long time to make a self. Tocqueville quotes Pascal saying that "the great advantage of being well-born is that it sets a man on his way by the age of eighteen or twenty, while another man may have to wait until he is fifty to get that far, thus yielding a gain of thirty years without effort." Agreeing, Tocqueville adds that "those thirty years are what ambitious men in democracies ordinarily must do without." The struggle to achieve financial security and success can also wear men out, so that "by the time they are able to do extraordinary things, they have lost the taste for them." The mediocrity built into democratic society alarms him. "What is most to be feared, it seems to me, is that the spark and grandeur of ambition might be swallowed up by the ceaseless petty occupations of private life, and that the human passions might subside and diminish at the same time, leaving society looking more tranquil but also less impressive as time goes by."

Tocqueville's views on ambition apply across the board: in the arts, in eloquence, in war—the worry is that everywhere, under democracy, men and women will turn inward, cultivating their own gardens, mindful chiefly of the present and careless of the future, attending only to private life and abandoning public life. His concern is that, owing to this concentration on private life, despotism will be given a considerable latitude—that citizens in democracies will be lashed to a servitude that they will scarcely notice but which will not be the less constraining for all that.

Behind Tocqueville's love of liberty, his worry about its reduction and ultimate loss, everywhere expressed in *Democracy in America*, is a deep-seated fear of the loss of freedom—or, more precisely, the surrender of freedom without a struggle. The new despotism he describes "likes to see the citizens enjoy themselves, provided that they think of nothing but enjoyment. It gladly works for their happiness but wants to be sole agent and judge of it. It provides for their security, foresees and supplies their necessities, facilitates their pleasures, manages their principal concerns, directs their industry, makes rules for their testaments, and divides their inheritances. Why should it not entirely relieve them from the trouble of thinking and all the cares of living?"

One of the chief reasons Tocqueville is opposed to centralization is that in it, too, he sees a loss of autonomy, which is itself the surest road to political oppression. As he writes near the end of Volume 2 of *Democracy,* "If despotism were to establish itself in today's democratic nations, it would probably have a different character. It would be more extensive and more mild, and it would degrade men without tormenting them." And it would be likely to arrive through centralization, for everywhere Tocqueville looked in Europe he found that administration had "become not only more centralized but also more inquisitive and minute. Everywhere it meddles more than of old in private affairs. It controls in its own fashion more actions and more of their details, and ever increasingly takes its place beside and above the individual, helping, advising, and constraining him."

While Tocqueville is utterly clear that the day of aristocracy is done, never to return, what he continues to admire about it is the leeway, made possible by the liberty aristocrats insisted upon for their own class, it gave to large ambitions, splendid dreams, grand actions. Under democracy, the danger is that the sovereign—which in democratic republics usually but not always means the sovereignty of the people—"does not break men's wills but softens, bends, and guides them ... does not destroy things but prevents them from coming into being ... inhibits, represses, saps, stifles, and stultifies, and in the end ... reduces each nation to nothing but a flock of timid and industrious animals, with the government as its shepherd."

What Tocqueville desired is democracy that was able if not to incorporate then at least to leave open the possibility for the best features of aristocracy: its civic, artistic, and military excellence. "The goal," as he writes, "is not to reconstruct an aristocratic society but to bring forth liberty from the midst of the democratic society in which God has decreed that we must live." His ideal was active political participation, action out in the public square. The politically inactive life was for Tocqueville a species of walking death. "It is indeed difficult to imagine how men who have entirely renounced the habit of managing their own affairs could be successful in choosing those who ought to lead them." For Tocqueville, the subjugating master is always waiting in the wings.

What Tocqueville so admired about the New England town meeting was that it forced everyone into active public life. What he admired about American voluntary associations was that they gave people a way to protect themselves from the encroachments of centralization by banding together to assert and protect their own interests—enlightened self-interest properly understood. "A political, industrial, commercial, or even scientific or literary association is an enlightened and powerful citizen that cannot be made to bow down at will or subjected to oppression in the shadows, and by defending its rights against the exigencies of power it saves common liberties." He admired the American jury system for, among other reasons, its educative function and its role in giving citizens firsthand experience of the administration of law.

In *Democracy in America,* Tocqueville expends more space proclaiming his love for liberty than actually defining it. "I should have loved liberty at all times, I think," he writes, "but at the present time I am inclined to worship it." But liberty for him is of at least two kinds: the negative liberty that frees people from the constraints of government and the positive liberty that allows them to get the best out of themselves and their talents. "It seems as though sovereigns nowadays are interested in men only to make great things with them," he writes. "I would rather that they gave a little more thought to making great men." Isaiah Berlin, in an essay on Georges Sorel, remarks that "the ideas of every philosopher concerned with human affairs in the end rest on his conception of what man is and can be." Tocqueville's conception, of man's, and of his own, possibilities, was high, much higher than he thought democracy, even at its best, was either interested in or capable of forming.

Although he does not often use the word "conformity," Tocqueville fears conformity of opinion under democracy. He cites cases where, in the United States, violence was used to ensure uniformity of opinion. But he is perhaps more concerned with the minor suppression that leads to major oppression, especially where moral pressure causes people holding dissenting opinions to suppress them out of fear of being placed beyond the social pale. In little things as in large, the condition of liberty is in danger of being limited, curbed, snuffed out. "I, for one, should be inclined to believe that liberty is less necessary in great things than in lesser ones if I thought that one could ever be assured of one without possessing the other."

Tocqueville ends *Democracy in America* on a half-minatory, half-hopeful note. He insists that nations, like men, are able to shape their own fate. "It is beyond the ability of nations today to prevent conditions within them from becoming equal, but it is within their power to decide whether equality will lead them into servitude or liberty, enlightenment or barbarism, prosperity or misery." He believed that "Providence has drawn a predestined circle around each man beyond which he cannot pass; but within those vast limits, man is strong and free; and so are peoples." If he felt that democracies were doomed, he tells us, "I would not have written this book. I would have confined myself to bewailing the fate of my fellow men in private.... I chose to speak out publicly about the dangers that equality poses to human independence because I firmly believe that those perils are the most formidable that the future holds, as well as the least anticipated. But I do not believe that they are insurmountable." He also held that "equality is less lofty, perhaps, but more just [than what has gone before], and its justice is the source of its grandeur and beauty."

Not everyone agrees that *Democracy in America* is a great book, but there can be no question that it is an amazing one. Royer-Collard, after reading the first volume, describing it in a letter to a friend, wrote: "To find a work to compare with it you have to go back to Aristotle's *Politics* and [Montesquieu's]

Spirit of the Laws." Tocqueville's second part, published in 1840, was not greeted with the same resounding applause that the first volume received. He wrote about this to Royer-Collard, striking his familiar note of self-doubt: "I am not deceived that, when it comes to the great public, I say great by number, the book is little read and badly known. This silence distresses me. It forces me to make an agonizing reappraisal of my position. I wonder if there is indeed something of worth in the work. I am often brought to doubt it, and this doubt leads me to wonder if the ability that some were kind enough to see is to be found in me. Because, that a man who has some ability should spend four years of his life doing a book without merit, that is not to be supposed."

What stirred this doubt in Tocqueville must have been his concern about honoring the complexity of his subject, for that is the first criterion of success for any good writer, and in the case of *Democracy in America* the subject itself was of a complexity of the highest magnitude. The book called for someone who could manipulate both the telescope and the microscope—who had, that is to say, mastery over both the distant and close-up view. The book Tocqueville set out to write could be done, but never, finally, to satisfaction, or at least to the satisfaction of a writer with Tocqueville's high standard. He had earlier written to Royer-Collard: "The subject is so difficult that it drives me to despair. I find it difficult to deal with ideas that have not yet been treated by anyone, but even much more difficult to restate completely, reasonably, and with some novelty a large number of things that have already been glimpsed or roughly portrayed by others. In a picture as vast as the one I want to paint, parts are necessarily encountered that are not new. I cannot omit them without doing harm to the overall view, and it is a laborious and often thankless task to deal with them. In short, I hope not to do worse than the first time."

Commentators have found much to criticize in *Democracy in America,* which since its publication has been scrutinized with Talmudic intensity and thoroughness. One unanswerable criticism of the work is how little Tocqueville's observations are based on statistical, or what is sometimes referred to as empirical, matter. His lack of interest in even the mildest of economic calculations, or indeed any of the material bases of American life, has been noted. The American historian Sean Wilentz thinks Tocqueville was intellectually in the pocket of the Federalists, who were among his chief respondents during his American visit, and that they gave him an anti-Jacksonian view of the United States. Garry Wills thinks Tocqueville never shook off his aristocratic bias but set himself out, falsely, as a neutral social scientist, while bringing the strong animus of an aristocrat to his study of democracy. Others have criticized Tocqueville for relying too heavily on the New England town meeting as his model for the active democratic life in America, some being uncharitable enough to point out that he himself never attended such a meeting. Another standard, more general criticism is that he came at things at too high a level of generality.

In a draft version of his book, Tocqueville wrote: "So physical causes contribute less to the maintenance of institutions than laws; laws less than mores." By mores, he wrote in the first volume of *Democracy in America,* "I mean here what the Ancients meant by the term: I apply it not only to mores in the strict sense, what one might call habits of the heart, but also to the various notions men might possess, to the diverse opinions that are current among them, and to the whole range of ideas that shape habits of the mind.... Thus I use this word to refer to the whole moral and intellectual state of a people." Yet the pages of the second volume of *Democracy in America* tend to be relatively bereft of particular mores. By then, Tocqueville was traveling fast, and couldn't stop for too long anywhere in his book.

John Stuart Mill, a year younger than Tocqueville but already regarded as the great English philosopher of his generation, reviewed both volumes of *Democracy in America*: the first in the *London and Westminister Review* (1835), the second in the *Edinburgh Review* (1840). Mill described the work as "the first philosophical book ever written on Democracy, as it manifests itself in modern society; a book, the essential doctrines of which it is not likely that any future speculations will subvert, to whatever degree they may modify them; while its spirit, and the general mode in which it treats its subject, constitute the beginning of a new era in the scientific study of politics." Mill also salutes Tocqueville for the impartiality of his book: "Not a trace of prejudice, or so much as a previous leaning either to the side of democracy or aristocracy, shows itself in his work."

Yet Mill lobs a number of well-placed grenades into Tocqueville's grand intellectual edifice. Early in his review of the first volume, he notes that Tocqueville is imprecise in saying that the "democratic principle is carried out in America to its utmost length," so long as the country has so many slaves and continues to deny women any active participation in public life, for Mill was an early and lifelong champion of women's rights.

Everyone, even among his admirers, will find in Tocqueville something he cannot abide. His high opinion of lawyers as the natural aristocrats of the American polity happens to be my own sticking point. Not all that many of the founding fathers, after all, were lawyers, and though two of the greatest Americans (Abraham Lincoln and Oliver Wendell Holmes Jr.) were lawyers by training, as a type lawyers have long fallen below the first class in America. So it is good to find Mill, contra Tocqueville (who was himself of course a lawyer), writing that "if the minds of lawyers were not, both in England and America, almost universally perverted by the barbarous system of technicalities—the opprobrium of human reason—which their youth is passed in committing to memory, and their manhood in administering—we think, with our author that they are the class in whom superiority of instruction, produced by superior study, would most easily obtain the stamp of general recognition; and that they would be the natural leaders of a people destitute of a leisured class." And, Mill goes on to say, this is also true of a learned class. He, for one, is grateful that England still has both a leisure class and a learned class from which to draw its leaders, and thus does not have to rely on lawyers.

Mill also attacks Tocqueville's notion of the tyranny of the majority, except where it comes to tyranny of opinion, and he later undermines the notion that democracy cannot exist without the presence of an aristocracy and a large peasant class, both of which also then existed in England. Equality of condition was not what made for the revolution of the day, as Mill understood it. What did was the rise of the middle, or commercial, class, which was growing into preponderance. Mill takes this to be Tocqueville's major confusion, arguing that "M. de Tocqueville then has, at least apparently, confounded the effects of Democracy with the effects of Civilization" by "letting it be supposed that he ascribes to equality of conditions several of the effects naturally arising from the mere progress of national prosperity."

Apropos of Tocqueville's speculations generally, Mill writes "that nothing on the whole comparable to them has yet been written upon democracy, will scarcely be disputed by any one who has read even our hasty abridgment of them. We must guard, at the same time, against attaching to these conclusions, or to any others that can result from such enquiries, a character of scientific certainty that can never belong to them. Democracy is too recent a phenomenon, and of too great a magnitude, for any one who now lives to comprehend its consequences."

Despite the criticisms that can be made of it, *Democracy in America* remains the last work of historical analysis and political philosophy of its magnitude produced in Western culture. I have read the book three times: once when young because I knew it to be among the short list of books that all Americans who wish to consider themselves educated about their own country are required to read; a second time to write an introduction to a Bantam Classics edition of the work; and now a third time for this intellectual portrait of its author. After three close readings, I still don't feel that I have mastered it. This is one sign of a masterwork: one doesn't master Proust's *Remembrance of Things Past* or Tolstoy's *War and Peace* either. Instead one draws continuous but always changing intellectual pleasure and nourishment from it. Another sign of a masterwork is that, after no matter how many rereadings, one is always finding new things in it, or is at least struck afresh by things one seems to have glided by too quickly on earlier readings. Only on my third reading of *Democracy in America,* for example, was I brought up by these two short sentences in the brief chapter in Volume 2 called "Why All Respectable Occupations Are Honorable in the United States": "The reason why so many wealthy Americans come to Europe is to avoid this obligation [faced by those who live in America] to work. In Europe they find the rubble of aristocratic societies in which idleness is still honored." Those sentences adumbrate the novelistic career of Henry James; the Americans Tocqueville here so briefly described are those who gave James his great international subject. James of course found the subject on his own—there is no evidence that he ever read Tocqueville—but Tocqueville spotted it first.

The differences between Volume 1 (1835) and Volume 2 (1840) of *Democracy in America* are the subject of an important article by the excellent Seymour Drescher. Volume 2, as noted, did not have the same resounding success as Volume 1. Tocqueville, in a letter to John Stuart Mill, stated his belief that "the comparatively weaker effect produced by" Volume 2 was owing to his attempt to "paint the general features of democratic societies of which no complete specimen yet exists." Volume 1 was more straightforward: it was anchored in a study of the particular political institutions of the United States. Volume 2 was more general, more speculative, and hence more arguable—also darker. Professor Drescher even wonders if "we may justifiably ask whether its author's conceptions of the state, of society, of the individual, and of their historical tendencies did not change so greatly between the publication of the two parts as to render them two different works."

The emphasis on the United States, as noted, is much less in the second volume; America and its *moeurs* are dropped in chiefly to illustrate larger points. New phrases are brought into play: "democratic centuries" are contrasted with "aristocratic centuries"; "individualism" is called into service, generally in a pejorative sense, usually to mean egotism, or to connote the privatization of life.

In the first volume, the mechanics of political institutions are analyzed, and the details of historical circumstances described: "The United States should render thanks to heaven for having so placed them up to now that they have need of neither standing armies, nor public force, nor a skillful and sustained foreign policy. If every one of these three necessities presents itself one can predict, without being a prophet, that they will lose their liberty or will concentrate power further." But the second volume deals more in those much less graspable realms of feelings, ideas, and values.

In Tocqueville's second volume England comes more to the

fore for comparative uses, probably for the good reason that Tocqueville had twice visited England, in 1833 and in 1835. But the overall optimistic tone of Volume 1 begins to fade decisively in Volume 2. What Drescher calls the "wild child" of democracy of 1835 "has become the timid child" of 1840, "weak, selfish, stagnating."

Tocqueville wrote Volume 2 of *Democracy in America* during a time when people were retiring more and more into their private lives. Among the voters in his district, he found a self-absorption and want of interest in public life that dried up all civic feeling. What Tolstoy called "family egotism"—the world can go to hell, just so that everything is all right with my little André—seemed more and more prevalent. Europe was undergoing a wave of industrialism, and Tocqueville saw danger here, too: the danger of an economic aristocracy—a plutocracy, really—crueler than any that had gone before. Unlike the commercial spirit of America, which thrived on liberty, industrial organization meant the accumulation of power in fewer and fewer hands. In the France of Louis-Philippe, political associations were limited, and new restraints had been put on the press. Centralization meanwhile was growing both in France and in England, and Tocqueville increasingly saw a stronger and stronger connection between it and despotism. Although he did not use the word, "bureaucracy" was more and more becoming the enemy. (Here, of course, he anticipated the great German sociologist Max Weber.) The squalor of political life under Louis-Philippe, which Tocqueville witnessed firsthand as a member of the Chamber of Deputies, no doubt further darkened his views.

"If [the five years between the publication of Volume 1 and Volume 2] brought Tocqueville to a new image of democratic man," Seymour Drescher writes, "it was mainly because the consciousness of the author reacted to the changing climate of his own community. In this sense [the second volume of *Democracy in America*] was as empirical as its predecessor."

If Tocqueville's views had become darker, the intellectual horizon of the second volume of *Democracy in America* is wider, the moral passion more prevalent and deeper. If the first volume is a significant work of political science and sociology, the second ascends from there to become something larger: a major work of political philosophy.

Chapter Seven

EVEN BEFORE the reviews were in on his second volume, Tocqueville had decided, perhaps partly because of the exhaustion brought on by writing so complex a work, to put an end to his career as a writer. On November 20, 1938, he wrote to Royer-Collard: "I don't think I'm deceiving myself ... when I say that nothing has been or is more contrary to my inclinations than to assume the position of an author in the world. That is entirely opposed to my way of judging the things that matter in this life. My firm wish, therefore, after this book is finished, and whatever its fate may be, is to work for myself and not to write for the public anymore, unless a very important and *very natural* occasion for doing so presents itself, which is unlikely."

Tocqueville would go on to write two more books: one, *Recollections*, his eyewitness account of the Revolution of 1848, he arranged to have published posthumously; the other, *The Old Regime and the Revolution*, he left half done. Both are considerable works—from a purely literary point of view, *Recollections* is my own favorite of his writings—but it is on *Democracy in America* that, more than 175 years after he wrote it, Tocqueville's reputation as a major political thinker stands today. And at least in part, this is owing to Tocqueville's reputation as a clairvoyant, a seer, a prophet.

This reputation was one Tocqueville claimed not to seek. He did write in his introduction to *Democracy in America* that he "wished to consider the whole future." At the same time, he was suspicious of those who thought themselves in possession of knowledge of the distant future in politics. To Harriet Grote, wife of the English classicist George Grote, he reported, "History teaches me that none of the men who have been present at the destruction of religious or social organizations that the world has already seen, could foretell or even imagine what was to follow: this has not prevented Christianity from succeeding idolatry, domestic service from succeeding slavery, the barbarians from succeeding Roman civilization, and feudal hierarchy from succeeding barbarism. Each of these changes took place without having been foreseen, least of all by any of the writers ... who have lived in the time that immediately preceded, and before the fundamental revolution." Elsewhere he wrote: "I think it highly imprudent for man, who each day fails to grasp what is real and present and who is constantly surprised by the unexpected in the things he knows best, to try to prescribe the limits of the possible and judge the future."

That Tocqueville nonetheless wanted to influence the future—to steer it, in the instance of France—in the direction of intelligent accommodation to the new democracy, is not in doubt. George Wilson Pierson writes that "he took no pleasure in prophesying for its own sake. The role of Cassandra held too little appeal for him." But he did so when necessary, through presenting his often dour premonitions, in the hope that they might alter men's faulty plans and heedless behavior as they stumbled into the future. As Pierson put it, he did want "to foretell, but partly also because he wanted to forewarn, and to forewarn in time."

James Bryce, who took up the Tocquevillian task of describing American political institutions, asserted, in his essay "Hamilton and Tocqueville," that "history teaches nothing more plainly than the vanity of predictions in the realm of what we call the moral and political sciences, in religion, in ethics, in sociology, in government and politics.... Observers keen enough to interpret the underlying phenomena of their own time may help us by showing which of the tendencies now at work are likely to become ruling factors in the near future. But beyond the near future—that is to say, beyond the lifetime of the generation which already holds power—no true philosopher will venture."

Tocqueville did so venture, frequently and daringly, and with an impressively high percentage of accuracy. The new condition of equality called for a new political science, he said. ("Political science," a bad old joke has it, with the science understood as in Christian Science, which is to say not very scientific at all.) One of the tests of any science is its predictive power. Santayana notes that "causation isn't a law, but an observable derivation of fact from fact in particular instances." Although he was often accused of a priori reasoning, Tocqueville was especially brilliant at linking facts together, and drawing persuasive conclusions from the linkages; and from these conclusions predictions naturally followed.

Why did Tocqueville bother at all with making predictions about the United States and democracy? To enhance the allure of his book? To increase his own authority? To establish the scientific standing of his thought? Because it was in his nature to do so? This last reason is the one I favor above the others. Tocqueville's was a mind that tended toward generalization, and a well-made generalization, if it is to hold up, ought to hold up for the past, present, and future—for all time. A young American surrealist poet, Dean Young, writes: "Everyone should study history because the present is too / complicated and no one knows a fucking thing about the future." If Tocqueville, who had the contemplative disease to a very high power, were to have believed that, he would have had to slash his wrists.

Tocqueville's generalizations also have a suggestibility about them that carries a reader into the future even when Tocqueville isn't offering a prediction at all. "Democracy relaxes social bonds but tightens natural bonds. It brings kin closer together while at the same time driving citizens further apart," he wrote in his second volume of *Democracy in America*. The first question one asks of any generalization is, of course, Is it true? Was it true at the time it was cast? follows, leading on to, Is it likely to be true in the future? In the instance of this particular generalization, the answer to all three questions is yes. In fact, the generalization is truer now than when Tocqueville wrote it. One looks about in the United States today and discovers Americans more and more circling their wagons around their families, with child rearing becoming ever more central and time-consuming in the lives of young couples. The family has become a tighter and tighter social unit, cohesive above all others and often excluding most others—and certainly more and more excluding public life.

"The passion for material well-being is essentially a middle-class passion," Tocqueville writes. He notes that aristocrats do not enjoy physical comfort any less than the middle class does; but because aristocrats have been born to it, acquiring it does not become a preoccupation for them, as is the tendency in the middle class. "For them [aristocrats], therefore, material well-being is not the purpose of life. It is a way of living." Anyone with the least social acuity cannot have failed to notice that, with the increase of middle-class affluence in America, consumer goods of all kinds have taken on a more central role, so central that the phrase "consumer society" as a description of America, hackneyed though it has become, still absorbs a fair amount of truth.

"In the United States, religious zeal never ceases to warm itself at patriotism's hearth," Tocqueville writes, leading one instantly to think of the active participation of evangelical Christians in politics in our day. "While the natural instincts of democracy lead the people to banish distinguished men from power, an instinct no less powerful leads distinguished men to shun careers in politics, in which it is so very difficult to remain entirely true to oneself or advance without self-abasement." True then, and perhaps even truer now, as anyone must conclude who considers the very brief roster of genuinely extraordinary men in American political life over the last 100 years or so. Time and again this happens in *Democracy in America:* true then, one says to oneself; true now; likely to be true for decades to come.

In one of his chapters on the military and war and peace in democracies, Tocqueville writes: "There are two things that will always be difficult for a democratic people to do: to start a war and to finish it." He thought this was so because democracy cannot maintain idealism for too long a stretch; those who live under it put prosperity and material well-being above all else. Democracies can successfully fight only defensive wars. The United States has been fortunate in thus far never having to fight such a war. In the matter of offensive or strategic wars, think how late the United States was in entering World War I. Think, again, how much effort Franklin Delano Roosevelt had to put into selling World War II to the American people. Only the Japanese attack on Pearl Harbor clinched the sale; and the draft, which sent a wide variety of Americans to fight the war, was chiefly responsible for encouraging Americans at home, almost all of whom had relatives or friends in the war, to make the sacrifices necessary to continue it. Harry S. Truman was often on the ropes in defending his decision to send troops into Korea. In Vietnam, the United States did not so much start a war as slip into it; and bringing it to an end proved one of the most dismal episodes in twentieth-century American history. America's recent war in Iraq is yet another instance of the complications entailed in taking up the offensive in a democracy. Once again, Tocqueville nails it.

In the realm of more precise predictions, Tocqueville, despite his averred nervousness about prophesying the future, was dauntless. "I believe that the Indian race in North America is doomed," he writes in the first volume of *Democracy in America,* and who is to say, the millions made from casinos on Indian reservations to the contrary notwithstanding, he was not right? Tocqueville was sympathetic to the Indian population in America, and because his sympathy was imaginative, it was of the best kind. He had something of the same sympathy great novelists feel for their characters. In the case of the Indians he knew what was being lost. The portrait he paints of the American Indian in *Democracy in America* and elsewhere in his writing tends to be one of natural majesty defeated and sadly degraded.

"If forced to make a prediction about the future, I would say that it is highly likely that abolition of slavery in the South will increase the hostility of the southern white population toward Blacks." The accuracy of this prediction, too, is high. It was high during Reconstruction, it was high during the years of integration and the civil rights movement, and it does not seem all that much lower today.

Tocqueville knew that race was the great question mark in the destiny of the United States. In *Democracy in America,* he argued persuasively about how deleterious slavery was not only to slaves but to their owners, economically, temperamentally, and not least morally. He predicted the abolition of slavery, and did so because he knew its continuation simply wasn't feasible. He failed to predict the Civil War, and might even be said to have miscalled it, when he wrote: "It can therefore be accepted as a general truth that in centuries of equality civil wars will become much rarer and much shorter."

He also did not so much predict as suggest the possibility that the United States might one day see a war between blacks and whites. He was, of course, wrong about this, though in the late 1960s, with the race riots in Watts, in Newark, on the west side of Chicago, and elsewhere, the possibility that this prediction would become true seemed harrowingly near. Close but, thank God, no cigar for Tocqueville here.

Tocqueville predicted that the northern ethos, spirit, and industrial organization would one day also dominate in the South. The southern United States "will end ... by being dominated by the North.... The situation of the North therefore seems destined to become the common measure to which everything else [in the South] must adjust," he predicted, again rightly. Think how Atlanta, Georgia, once the most southern of cities, now a major location for corporate headquarters, has today become northern in its organization and increasingly northern in its tone and general feeling.

Notably for his day, Tocqueville, snobbish though he may have been in some regards, had not a scintilla of racism. "What is happening in the South," Tocqueville wrote in *Democracy in America*, "strikes me as both the most horrible and the most natural consequence of slavery." By this he meant both the mistreatment of blacks and the ultimate degradation of the morale of southern whites. He went on to say that his "indignation" as well as all his "hatred is reserved for those who, after more than a thousand years of equality [induced by Christian belief], introduced servitude into the world once more."

In the second volume of *Democracy in America,* Tocqueville predicted the swings in business cycles likely to visit democracies: "Recurrent industrial crises are, I believe, an endemic malady of democratic nations today. This malady can be made less dangerous, but it cannot be cured, because it is due not to an accident but to the very temperament of the people in question." The rise of taxes in the United States, to the level of taxes under European monarchies and aristocracies, was another of his correct predictions. He was wrong—perhaps only half wrong—in saying that Americans would never stand for conscription: "Compulsory recruitment is so contrary to the ideas and so foreign to the habits of the people of the United States that I doubt whether anyone would ever dare put it into law." It was put into law during World War II and for a while afterward, but conscription is not likely to be instituted soon again, and certainly not likely to be instituted easily.

Tocqueville predicted that the working classes would want—nay, demand—greater equality. He predicted the same of African-Americans. (He also, elsewhere, said that the Irish would fight for their freedom against the English.) But he failed to predict that women, too, would want the vote and all the equality that followed naturally from their obtaining it.

As a connoisseur of revolution, he predicted that revolution is most likely at precisely the time when despotic governments ease their hold on people and liberalize their policies, suggesting a revolution of rising expectations. This is of course precisely what happened in Russia before the Bolshevik revolution; as the czar became more liberal, revolutionary ardor heated up. As mentioned earlier, Tocqueville predicted that one day the United States and Russia would vie for hegemony over the world. One cannot resist adding here that not one among the large number of American and European Sovietologists, professional students of the Soviet Union, predicted the end of communism there.

In the realm of culture, Tocqueville said that in the United States "most people who attend plays go in search of intense emotions of the heart rather than pleasures of the intellect. True then, true now, and a fine gloss on William Dean Howells's remark that what Americans want is "a tragedy with a happy ending." Tocqueville also predicted the rise of the auto-biographical element in the poetry of democratic people, a call so prescient that it might serve as an introduction to American poetry, from Walt Whitman to Robert Lowell: "I celebrate myself, and sing myself."

Tocqueville predicted that religions under democracy would increasingly drop their forms: "A religion that became more obsessive about details, more inflexible, and more concerned with petty observances at a time when men were becoming more equal would soon find itself reduced to a band of fanatical zealots surrounded by an incredulous multitude." Toss out the Latin Mass, bring on the guitars.

Perhaps above all, Tocqueville was correct when he saw that the reigning issue for modern societies under democracy, and one that would continue to face them, was to be found in the necessary and continuing rivalry between equality and liberty. Whatever arrangements are made to ensure equality, they can be made only at the price of withdrawing some degree of liberty. Cut liberty loose and equality is unlikely to be well served: consider, in our own day, free markets, which favor, at least temporarily, the strong over the weak; the already rich over the poor; and, yes, the educated over the uneducated. One would like to think there is some middle way between liberty and equality, and sometimes there is, but just as often the two are in unresolvable conflict; presented with a clear fork in the road—equality this way, liberty that—no society can take both simultaneously. Tocqueville was the first to see that this was the premier issue brought to the fore by the new democracy, and what he saw remains no less pertinent in our day and will probably be pertinent for all days to come.

Brilliant though so many of Tocqueville's predictions now seem, his miscalls, which were not negligible, deserve mention, lest he take on the aura of Nostradamus. First among Tocqueville's incorrect predictions was his belief that the federal government would be likely to wither away with the natural enlargement of territory and population in the United States. He saw this as well on its way to happening: "A careful study of the history of the United States over the last forty-five years," he wrote in *Democracy in America*, "readily convinces one that federal power is decreasing." Quite the reverse was to occur:

the larger and more spread out the population, the more federal government was required to build roads, regulate commerce, enforce laws involved in interstate crimes, and much more. Tocqueville was led into this error by his reading in *The Federalist,* but also by his belief that Americans of 1830s felt more loyalty to their states or regions than to the Union. True though that may have been early in the nineteenth century, it began to be much less so by that century's end.

Majorities' enforcing their will on minorities was another of Tocqueville's abiding worries about democracy. At first he thought this might come about through strictly political means—that is, through legislatures—but by the time he wrote his second volume he thought it more likely to be exerted through public opinion crushing different or even oddly angled views in favor of those upheld by the great mass. Only in the second volume of *Democracy in America* did Tocqueville avail himself of the phrase "tyranny of the majority." James Bryce felt that Tocqueville was largely mistaken here, writing that "the tyranny of the majority is not a serious evil to the America of today, though people still sometimes profess alarm at it." Yet one wonders if Bryce read Hawthorne's *The Scarlet Letter,* the great American novel whose very theme is the tyranny of the majority; certainly he did not live to see the era of Joseph McCarthy, when a putative majority wreaked its own (short-lived, limited, but quite real) menace. If Tocqueville was not perfectly correct, the point nonetheless remains, if only by way of prophylaxis, a useful one on which to be wrong.

Tocqueville's gift of prophecy, such as it was, then, wasn't really a gift at all. When he provided a prediction, it was generally based on an analysis of the materials made with a rigor that permitted him to understand the past and the present, and hence to have strong intuitions about the future, of the subject.

If Tocqueville may be accused of a priori reasoning, or drawing his conclusions not from empirical data but from preconceptions, then it ought to be said that his preconceptions were of a high and richly complex order. "Human institutions can be changed," he wrote, "but man cannot." He never took human beings as wiser than they are, but neither did he think they were clay made for easy molding. He knew that self-interest was never to be discounted (and thus that, in the business culture dominating America, commerce trumped politics), so he could confidently predict the unlikelihood of a revolution in the United States. "I know of nothing more opposed to revolutionary mores than commercial mores," he wrote.

Tocqueville understood that human beings were—sometimes separately, sometimes simultaneously—serious and foolish ("I marvel at the imbecility of human reason," he wrote), grand and petty, ambitious and hopelessly lazy, adventurous and security-minded. Institutions played off human nature, and human nature off institutions. Yet his model of human nature was never permanently fixed. "In centuries of equality the human mind takes on a different cast. It is easy to imagine that nothing stays put. The mind is possessed by the idea of instability ... for in democratic centuries, when everything is in flux, the most mobile thing of all is the human heart."

For Tocqueville, the conviction that "the search for absolute demonstrable truth, like the search for perfect happiness, was an effort after the impossible" didn't mean that the great questions ought to be abandoned. "What do you want from society and government?" he wrote in the first volume of *Democracy in America*. Clarity on this point was essential:

Do you wish to impart a certain loftiness to the human mind, a generous way of looking at things of this world? Do you want to inspire in men a kind of contempt for material goods? Do you hope to foster or develop profound convictions and lay the groundwork for deep devotion?

Is your goal to refine mores, elevate manners, and promote brilliance in the arts? Do you want poetry, renown, and glory?

Do you seek to organize a people so as to act powerfully on all other peoples? Would you have them embark on enterprises so great that, no matter what comes of their efforts, they will leave a deep impression on history?

If, in your view, these are the main objectives that men in society ought to set for themselves, do not choose democratic government, for it offers no guarantee that you will reach your goal.

But if it seems useful to you to turn man's intellectual and moral efforts to the necessities of material life and use them to improve his well-being; if reason strikes you as more profitable to man than genius; if your purpose is to create not heroic virtues but tranquil habits; if you would rather see vice than crime and are prepared to accept fewer great deeds in exchange for fewer atrocities; if, instead of a brilliant society as a stage for your actions, you are willing to settle for a prosperous one; and if, finally, the principal purpose of a government is not, in your view, to make the nation as a whole as glorious or powerful as can be but to achieve for each individual the greatest possible well-being while avoiding misery as much as possible, then equalize conditions and constitute a democratic government.

Who, so many years later, is to say that in this complex formulation of political choice Alexis de Tocqueville was wrong? Right or wrong, *Democracy in America* always provokes in the most useful way. "The books which have made men reflect the most, and have had the greatest influence on their opinions and their acts, are those in which the author did not seek to dictate dogmatically what it was proper to think," Tocqueville wrote to his friend Francisque de Corcelle in 1853, "but rather where he pointed them in the direction of truths for them to find, as if of themselves." In *Democracy in America,* he had himself written precisely such a book.

Chapter Eight

TOCQUEVILLE WON his first official claim to powers of prophecy in January of 1848. In a speech to the Chamber of Deputies, he not only predicted the Revolution of 1848 but called it on the button. The speech itself took some courage to deliver. In it he told his fellow deputies that they did not exist beyond their own self-interest, were devoid of public spirit, and did not in any way deserve to lead. His "somber prophecies," Tocqueville recounts, "were received with insulting laughter by the majority." Charles de Rémusat recalls Thiers leaning over to whisper to him of Tocqueville, "What a nasty little man," and making a disparaging remark about his pallor.

Tocqueville also told his fellow deputies that they were slumbering on a volcano. He couldn't say with precision when, but soon the workers would take to the streets. "For the first time in, perhaps, sixteen years there is a feeling, a conscious-ness of instability, and that is a feeling which goes before revolutions, often announcing them and sometimes bringing them about, and that feeling is there to a very serious extent across the country."

Public mores, he announced, were now dominated by the spirit of private advantage. "Note that I do not say this as a moralist, but as a politician; do you know what is the general, effective, deep cause that makes private mores turn corrupt? It is the change in public mores. It is because morality does not prevail in the main acts of life, that it does not find its way down into the least important ones."

Not the government alone but the entire governing class, by which Tocqueville meant the middle class, brought this about. "The real cause, the effective cause, which makes men lose power is that they have become unworthy to wield it." This sentence whipped up his audience even more. "I told you just now that this ill sooner or later—I do not know how or whence it will come, but sooner or later—will bring about the most serious revolution in this country; make no mistake about that."

Sooner rather than later, the revolution arrived. At ten o'clock at night on February 23, on the boulevard des Capucines, before the Foreign Ministry, soldiers, goaded perhaps by the pistol shot of an agent provacateur, or perhaps by that of a soldier thinking his commanding officer was about to be attacked by a worker with a torch—no one knows for certain—fired into a crowd of protesting workers shouting for reform, killing sixteen of them and wounding many more. Thus flew the spark that ignited the conflagration. The mob put the bloodied corpses on a tumbril and paraded with them to the working-class district of Saint-Antoine; as they marched, they cried out that those in power were murdering the people, and demanded vengeance.

Events moved quickly after that. Guizot was dismissed as head of Louis-Philippe's current government and went into exile; many defections were discovered among the National Guard; and Louis-Philippe's advisers, fearing danger, strongly suggested that he depart the capital for his home in Saint-Cloud. The next day, the workers took to the streets of Paris. Universal suffrage was proclaimed by a provisional government. (Hitherto to be able to vote, one had been required to pay direct taxes of 200 francs, which meant that less than 1 percent of the French ever voted—just 241,000 men in a population of roughly 30 million.) Freedom of the press and assembly and the right to work were proclaimed. Crowds gathered at night on the streets; a threat of menace hung over the city. Louis-Philippe was made nervous when he heard the National Guard assigned to guard him at the Tuileries shouting the same slogans as the mob: *Vive la réforme!* The editor of *La Presse*, a paper hitherto friendly to the government, wrote that the king must step down or expect to share the fate of Louis XVI. No doubt feeling the tickle of the guillotine's blade at his neck, Louis-Philippe abdicated, fleeing Paris with his family in three small carriages. The Chamber of Deputies was dissolved. France's Second Republic was in business.

Flaubert, in the first chapter of part three of his novel *Sentimental Education*, recounts, through the eyes of his young hero Frédéric Moreau, what he elsewhere called the "genius for disorder" of the street crowds on February 24. Then twenty-seven years old, Flaubert was himself part of that crowd, and even though he claimed to have read more than twenty books about these events in preparation for his novel, for the most part he simply described what he had seen. Here is his rendering of the scene of the crowd at the Palais-Royal after the royal family has departed:

> The mob, less out of vengeance than from a desire to assert its supremacy, smashed or tore up mirrors, curtains, chandeliers, sconces, tables, chairs, stools—everything that was movable, in fact, down to albums of drawings and needlework baskets. They were the victors, so surely they were entitled to enjoy themselves. The rabble draped themselves mockingly in lace and cashmere. Gold fringes were twined round the sleeves of smocks, hats with ostrich plumes adorned the heads of blacksmiths, and ribbons of the Legion of Honor served as sashes for prostitutes. Everybody satisfied his whims; some danced, others drank. In the Queen's bedroom, a woman was greasing her hair with pomade; behind a screen a group of keen gamblers were playing cards....
>
> The palace was overflowing with people. Seven bonfires were blazing in the inner courtyard. Pianos, chests of drawers, and clocks were being thrown out of the windows. Fire engines were squirting water right up to the roofs. Some hooligans were trying to cut the hosepipes with their swords, and Frédéric urged a military cadet to intervene. The cadet did not understand,

and indeed seemed to be half-witted. All round, in the two arcades, the mob, after raiding the wine cellars, was abandoning itself to a horrifying orgy. Wine was flowing in torrents, wetting the people's feet, and ragamuffins were drinking out of the bottoms of broken bottles, shouting as they staggered about.

"In a riot, as in a novel," Tocqueville wrote, "the most difficult thing to invent is the ending." Tocqueville also recounted these and other events in *Recollections*, his memoir of the Revolution of 1848. In this book he set out his historiographical preferences. He claimed to hate "absolute system" histories, which assign all events to a few great causes—Zeitgeist, economic arrangements, legal institutions—and thereby banish the importance of human actions from history. Such histories also deny the role of chance in human affairs. Tocqueville's own view was that both men and accident had substantial roles to play in the fate of nations. "But," he wrote, "I am firmly convinced that chance can do nothing unless the ground has been prepared in advance. Antecedent facts, the nature of institutions, turns of mind, and the state of mores are the materials from which chance composes those impromptu events that surprise and terrify us."

He then lists, in the case of the 1848 Revolution, what these were: the industrial revolution, which brought many workers into Paris, not all of them able to live on their wages or to find work; the passion for material pleasures, which fed on envy; theories that poverty could be eliminated by mechanical changes in social arrangements; contempt, well earned, for the nation's rulers; centralization, which brought the engine house of the country to Paris; and the instability of a society that had lived through no fewer than seven revolutions within sixty years.

Tocqueville did not intend his *Recollections* for publication in his lifetime. (In fact, the book wasn't officially published until 1893, when his grandnephew brought it out, initially with many editorial deletions.) He claimed that he wrote the memoir for himself alone: "These pages are to be a mirror, in which I can enjoy seeing my contemporaries and myself, not a painting for the public to view. My best friends are not to know about them, for I wish to keep my freedom to describe myself and them without flattery. I want to uncover the secret motives that made us act, them and myself as well as other men, and, when I have understood these, to state them. In a word, I want to express myself honestly in these memoirs, and it is therefore necessary that they be completely secret." The only part of this interesting statement open to doubt is contained in the first sentence; nobody—certainly nobody with the literary gifts of Alexis de Tocqueville—writes so extended a composition without planning on its one day being read by a wide public.

In *Democracy in America* Tocqueville was operating at a fairly high level of generality. Few proper names are mentioned. Subjects are taken up for their general—one might even say generalizable—import. But in the *Recollections*, another side of Tocqueville is on display: the specialist in the human comedy, the writer with an eye for human weakness—which politics can bring out as few other things do.

Recollections is also a little handbook on revolution. Unlike the Bolshevik revolution of 1917, the Revolution of 1848 had no small band of leaders but was brought to life by a mob—an underpaid, unrepresented, hungry mob. "Usually," Tocqueville writes, "revolutions brought about by the emotions of the mob have been desired but not premeditated.... They spring spontaneously from some general malady of men's minds suddenly brought to a crisis by an unforeseen chance incident. And those who claim to be the originators and leaders of these revolutions do not originate or lead anything: their sole merit is identical with that of the adventurers who have discovered most of the unknown lands, namely the courage to go straight ahead while the wind blows." Revolutions, he thought, also provide a place for the literally insane: "I have always thought that in revolutions, especially democratic revolutions, madmen (not those metaphorically called such, but real madmen) have played a very considerable political part." In the pages of *Recollections* he will go on to describe a number of these maniacs.

Tocqueville is much impressed by the role of accident in this particular revolution. As for the story that the government was deliberately massacring the people, he writes: "I knew the vices of the July government [of Louis-Philippe] all too well, and cruelty was not among them. I consider it to have been of the most corrupt, but least bloodthirsty, that has ever existed, and I repeat that rumor [of the government murdering large numbers of people] only to show how such rumors help revolutions along." After meeting with a General Bedeau, who was flustered by the events of the day, Tocqueville remarks, "This did not surprise me, for I have always noticed that it is the military men who lose their heads first and show up as weakest in a revolutionary situation." He goes on to explain that warfare is relatively organized—with a clear enemy, strategies in place, tactics set out—and that troops are obedient in a way that an unruly revolutionary crowd never is.

The portraits of political figures in *Recollections* are among the abiding pleasures of what is generally a dark book. Tocqueville may not have suffered fools gladly, but he clearly took much pleasure in writing about them. He may not have been a humorous, but he was a distinctly witty, man, and few things brought out his wit better than contemplation of other men's pretensions and ambitions. Tocqueville writes that he must "admit that one's private feelings about men are a bad guide in politics." He intends to render cool judgments: no one, in other words, is to be spared.

Beginning at the top, he is death on King Louis-Philippe. The revolution "was *unforeseen* by everybody, but by him most of all; no warning from the outside had prepared him for it, for his mind had retreated long ago into the sort of haughty loneliness inhabited by almost all kings whose long reigns have been prosperous, who mistake luck for genius, and who do not want to listen to anybody, because they think they have no more to learn." Louis-Philippe's fault was "to corrupt the people without defying them and to twist the spirit of the Constitution without changing the letter; to play off the country's vices one against the other; and gently to drown revolutionary passion in the love of material pleasures; this had been his idea throughout his life, and it gradually became, not just his main, but his only thought." Louis-Philippe was a man who would "change his opinions less but his conduct more easily than any man I have ever known." Tocqueville had been in the king's company only once, when Louis-Philippe had asked him about America but had then proceeded to tell him about America and various other things. ("I had not said four words," Tocqueville notes.) Forty-five minutes later, the king rose, thanking Tocqueville for the pleasure of their conversation, "and dismissed me, clearly delighted with me as one usually is by anyone in whose presence one feels one has talked well."

Even the most minor figures do not get off without Tocqueville's skewering them in his brilliant prose portraits. Of a man named Auguste de Portalis, who would become attorney general of Paris, Tocqueville writes that "he had neither his uncle's brains and exemplary mores, nor his platitudinous piety. His coarse, violent, cross-grained mind readily absorbed every false idea and extreme opinion current in our day." Of Madame de Lamartine, wife of the poet-politician, he writes: "She had pretty well every defect that can be associated with virtue and, without altering its character, make it less agreeable. She had an imperious temper, great pride, and a mind that, although upright, was inflexible and sometimes harsh, so that it was impossible not to respect but equally impossible to like her." Tocqueville had a penchant for sentences with such trapdoor endings: one thinks he is setting out to praise someone, and then, bang!, the trapdoor opens and the victim falls into a pit of alligators.

The portraits of important figures are rendered in balanced, pointillist detail. "For although he was very intelligent," Tocqueville writes of Charles Duchâtel, minister of the interior, "he was limited; his intellect could clearly see each detail on its horizon, but could not imagine that the horizon might change. He was learned, distinguished, ardent, bilious and vindictive, a member of that scholarly clique that regulates its politics by imitating past examples and by its historical memory, confining its thought to a single idea, which both warms it and blinds it." Leonor Havin, later to be a commissioner of the republic, is "one of those footloose men of ambition who found themselves trapped for ten years in the opposition [to Louis-Philippe], whereas they had intended only to pass through that way. What a lot of men of that type I saw round me, tormented by their own virtue and in despair because the best part of their lives was spent in criticizing the vices of others without a chance to give play to their own, nourished by nothing but the imaginary abuses of power."

For all the chill criticism of Tocqueville's portraits, they are also fair. "I have never known a less sincere mind [than Lamartine's], or one that more completely despised the truth. When I say that he despised it, I am wrong; he never honored it enough to be concerned with it in any way at all. Talking or writing, he departed from truth and returned to it without taking any notice, being solely concerned with the particular effect he wanted to produce at that moment." A few pages later, though, comparing Lamartine with Ledru-Rollin, another key figure in the National Assembly during the revolution, he adds: "I had no more confidence in Lamartine's common sense than in his disinterestedness, and indeed thought him capable of anything except a cowardly act or a vulgar phrase." Ah, that final redeeming touch.

Generosity of judgment, inspired by dedication to truthfulness, even about people whom one otherwise finds disagreeable, is a mark of a superior mind. Before he renders his judgment of George Sand, whom he first met at a luncheon given by Richard Monckton Milnes, the English man of letters and social butterfly, Tocqueville remarks that he has no taste for "literary adventurers"; besides, he adds, "I had a strong prejudice against Madame Sand, for I detest women who write." And yet, seated next to George Sand at lunch, he discovers that "she charmed me. I found her features rather massive, but her expression wonderful; all her intelligence seemed to have retreated into her eyes, abandoning the rest of her face to raw matter. I was most struck at finding her with something of that naturalness of manner characteristic of great spirits. She really did have a genuine simplicity of manner and language, which was perhaps mingled with a certain affectation of simplicity in her clothes."

Finally, it is good for me, a Jew, to be able to report that Tocqueville, though no doubt sharing some of the prejudice of his social class, rose above anti-Semitism to take Jews, as he did everyone else, case by case, man by man. (A test, as is well known, that many great writers, from Shakespeare to T. S. Eliot, have failed.) Consider Michel Goudchaux, described as "a radical and a banker," of whom Tocqueville writes: "He did not look like a Jew, though he was one on both his mother's and his father's side, for he had round cheeks, thick red lips, and a plump, short body that made him look like a cook in a good family. It was impossible to be more vain, irascible, quarrelsome, and petulant or more easily moved than he. He was unable to discuss difficulties in the budget without bursting into tears; yet he was one of the most valiant little men one could meet." Tocqueville goes on to show Goudchaux fearless in the streets of Paris when they are part of a team deputized to speak to the National Guard. "I should like to go and fight a little," Goudchaux tells Tocqueville when their mission is accomplished, and promptly goes off to do so bravely. "He announced this in such martial tones, which contrasted oddly with his pacific appearance, that I could not restrain a smile."

Scores of such portraits appear in the pages of *Recollections*. Tocqueville's was a mind that needed to take as exact a measure as possible of every man and woman he met. If he had a keen eye for character, his sense of novelistic detail was not less. When Guizot appears at the Chamber of Deputies to announce his having been dismissed, "he entered with his firmest step and haughtiest bearing, silently crossed the gangway, and mounted the tribune, almost throwing his head over backward for fear of seeming to bow it." Jean Pierre Sauzet, the president of the Chamber of Deputies, "had handsome but undistinguished features, the dignity of a cathedral verger, and a large fat body with very short arms. When he was restless or upset, as he nearly always was, he would waggle his little arms convulsively in all directions like a drowning man." This same man, during the commotion caused in the Assembly when it was invaded by the proletariat, did not so much walk but "slid off the platform on which his chair was placed. I saw him pass, a shapeless mass, before my eyes; never would I have believed that fear could accelerate such a fat body so much, or, rather, suddenly transmogrify it into a sort of liquid."

Tocqueville claimed to distrust what he called the "literary spirit in politics," which for him "consists in looking for what is ingenious and new rather than for what is true, being fonder of what makes an interesting picture than what serves a purpose, being very appreciative of good acting and fine speaking without reference to the play's results, and, finally, judging by impressions rather than reasons." That spirit is of course very much with us today, when people apply aesthetic criteria to make what should be political and moral judgments, despising a politician for his poor grammar or taste or clothes or wife quite as much as for his ideas or actions. But Tocqueville, I think, was fortunate in never letting his own strong literary spirit conquer his sound political judgment. The two lived quite amiably side by side, giving *Recollections* standing as a work of literature and distinguishing Tocqueville as one of the great political writers of all ages.

Allied to Tocqueville's literary sensibility were his introspection, another quality rare in practicing politicians; and his self-honesty, a quality rarer still. After delivering a number of thumping good put-downs of colleagues in the Chamber of Deputies, he remarks, "It is only right that I should take the same liberties with myself as I have taken, and will often take again, with so many others."

He begins by saying that he breathed more freely after the revolution, for he was glad the old parliamentary arrangement, in which he had not flourished, was done in. Under the old Chamber of Deputies, neither his strengths nor his weaknesses stood him in good stead. "I was not sufficiently virtuous to command respect, but I had too much integrity to adapt myself to all those petty practices then necessary for quick success." He had little patience for things that—or people who—didn't truly interest him. Whether because of his poor eyesight, or his supreme boredom, or the ingrained hauteur of the aristocrat, he could not remember the names of many people who might have been important to his career. "It is not that I despise them, but I have little truck with them, feeling that they are like so many clichés. I respect them, for they make the world work, but they bore me profoundly."

He also knew that his fellow deputies found him as disagreeable as he found most of them. In the various party leaders in the Chamber of Deputies he discovered an utter absence of impartial love of disinterestedness, character, or enlightenment, rendering them "more or less equally unworthy to command." He thought of himself as existing in "a morose isolation as a distant and badly judged character. I was continually conscious that imaginary qualities and defects were attributed to me." He was aware that he was seen as underhanded, cunning on his own behalf, vindictive, and having a bitter temperament. He knew himself to be "full of self-mistrust," and the low opinion that many of his fellow deputies had of him didn't make things easier.

What made this "cruel misunderstanding" all the more difficult for Tocqueville was that, as he put it, "for no man is approval more healthy than for me, and no one needs public esteem and confidence more to help him rise to the actions of which he is capable." This weakness in him, he came to feel, stemmed from "a great pride as nervous and restless as the mind itself." He felt, too, that "I often glide between good and evil with a soft indulgence that borders on weakness; and my quickness to forget grievances seems more like a lack of spirit, an inability to suffer the memory of an affront, rather than any virtuous effort to efface such impressions." Tocqueville stood in need of no psychotherapy; he was his own best analyst. Only a cure, alas, eluded him.

His propensity for pessimism was often pointed out to him. "You always see the black side of everything," Beaumont said, when he reported to Tocqueville that the defection of the National Guard to the cause of the revolution meant the overthrow of all authority. Fear of revolution, with its promise of disorder and the further curbing of true liberty, brought out this dark streak in Tocqueville more emphatically than all else.

If Tocqueville feared revolution, he did not fear or in any way look down on "the people," as the revolutionaries were fond of calling themselves. The "people," he felt, were really the urban proletarians, egged on by ideologues; they did not include the farm and rural population, or all the simple Frenchmen straining after a decent living, whom he held in great respect. Tocqueville knew how hard the lives of the poor could be—he wrote, after all, *A Memoir on Pauperism*—and he worked to improve their lives in ways that would not redound against them, as, it might be said, certain American welfare programs in recent American history kept their recipients hostage for generations. He did, though, think "the people" were dangerous when their heads were filled with "vain theories and chimerical hopes," two items in which revolutionaries in all ages seem to specialize. He was for reform and change, but orderly reform and change, and detested the idea of outright struggle between "the Haves and the Have-Nots," a phrase he may have been the first to use, in his speech of January 27, 1848, the one warning of the revolution to come. He wished to lighten the public responsibility of the poor, establish institutions that would allow them to become more prosperous, and assist them in any way possible; and he formulated specific proposals to bring all these things about.

The idea of a country torn between those who "had nothing, united in common envy" and "those who had everything, united in common terror" was what he worried him. He thought many of the revolutionaries then on the scene quite mad. His description of Louis Blanquin, who was prominent among them, speaking before the Assembly on May 15 gives a notion of his revulsion: "Although I have never seen him again, the memory of him filled me with disgust and horror ever since. He had sunken, withered cheeks, white lips, and a sickly, malign, dirty look, like a pallid, moldy corpse; he was wearing no visible linen; an old black frock coat covered his lean, emaciated limbs tightly; he looked as if he had lived in a sewer and only just come out."

Despite the revolutionary background before which he lived out the first half of 1848, Tocqueville claimed during those days to feel "a sense of happiness I had not known before." He had, as he wrote, "no monarchical connections and no affection or regret for any princes; and I had no cause to defend except freedom and human dignity." He was now with good conscience a republican, and his only aim was to "protect the ancient laws of society against the innovators by using the new strength the republican principle could give to government; to make sure the will of the people of France triumphs over the passions and desires of the Paris working men, and in this way to conquer demagoguery by democracy." For the first time as an active politician, he was not in opposition, but in the mainstream, "with the current of a majority in the only direction that my tastes, reason, and conscience could approve."

The element of actual danger during the heightened days of the revolution appears not in the least to have daunted Tocqueville. If anything, it stirred the adventurer in him. As a young man, it will be recalled, he was ready to fight a duel. In North America, he had lived through shipwrecks and braved the wilds of upper Michigan on horseback. During the most fevered days and nights of the 1848 Revolution, he walked the streets of Paris, goaded by curiosity, never put off by fear. Going off to attend a festival of the people at the Champs de Mars, anticipating a riot, he quietly slipped two pistols into his pockets. In argument or in any other realm, no one ever successfully caused him to back down. "I am less afraid of danger than of doubt," he wrote, and it was so.

Chapter Nine

T OCQUEVILLE SPOKE of his pleasure in being free of the government of the July Monarchy, under which, in the Chamber of Deputies, he felt very much a man on the sidelines, alone with his sound principles. With the departure of King Louis-Philippe and the installation of a republic after the February Revolution of 1848, he began to glide slowly but genuinely closer to the center of the action. The possibility loomed, or so it began to seem, of his becoming at last a serious player.

One sign of this was his election to a committee of eighteen deputies to write a constitution for the new republic. Who could possibly have been better equipped to serve on such a committee than he, the man who had made a specialty of comparative government and who was himself the leading expert on the world's most famously successful living republic, the United States of America? Aristotle, Plato, Montesquieu, the authors of *The Federalist*, Tocqueville—these were the minds that had thought most trenchantly about the organization of government and the principles of governing. A great pity that the others weren't alive to serve with Tocqueville on this committee, though they too, in the end, would probably have felt quite as useless as he did.

"For my part," Tocqueville wrote in his *Recollections,* "I have never been so wretched in any other committee I have served on." The great questions did not get debated; the great issues did not get aired; the great problems were given the most superficial of solutions. And Alexis de Tocqueville, the subtlest mind in European political theory for more than a century, played a less than central role.

In recounting his work on the Committee for the Constitution, Tocqueville remarks that it was unfortunate that the committee met in late May 1848, for the fighting in the streets of Paris had not altogether subsided and was to pick up with greater intensity in June. The committee's members, in other words, met with the smell of gunpowder in their nostrils and an element of fear still in their hearts. "The thing that most effectively deprived the Committee of its freedom of mind was, one must admit," Tocqueville noted, "fear of outside events and the excitement of the moment." Had the committee met after the revolution was ended in June, a different atmosphere would have prevailed, and the likelihood is that a stronger document might have emerged. A year or so later, as Tocqueville wrote, "everybody wanted to get rid of the [new] Constitution, some by socialism, some by monarchy."

How could this have happened? Politics as usual and the

fallibility of human beings are the short answers. On the Committee for the Constitution, Tocqueville found himself ensnared in the normal work of politics: compromising where necessary, bartering positions where it made sense to do so, working around the vanities and special interests of other committee members. "Taking the Committee as a whole," Tocqueville notes, "it was easy to see that nothing very remarkable was to be expected from it," and he adds: "All this bore little resemblance to those men, so sure of their aim and so well acquainted with the best means to reach it, who drafted the American Constitution sixty years ago with Washington in the chair."

The first question before the committee was whether the new French republic ought to have one or two chambers. With the United States very much in mind, Tocqueville thought two chambers best; he believed that two chambers would provide for greater natural checks and balances. Part of his argument had to do with the notion that three government bodies—two assemblies and an executive—would do much to alleviate the natural conflict that might arise between a single assembly and a chief executive, who were likely to go at things head to head. "Nothing was certain," he felt, "except that they would wage war and thereby ruin the republic," as of course eventually happened. But owing largely to the fact that so many members of the committee were already used to a single-body assembly, and the general feeling that public opinion was against this change in arrangements, Tocqueville found himself in the fifteen-to-three minority on this question.

On the matter of how the president of the new republic

was to be elected— through popular vote or by election within the assembly—Tocqueville's own view was that "the president should not be directly elected by the citizens, but that that duty be entrusted to delegates elected by the people." Once again he had taken his ideas on the subject, he reports, "from the Constitution of the United States [with its electoral college]. I don't think anyone would have noticed that, had I not mentioned it, so little prepared was the committee for the great part it had to play." Tocqueville lost on this question, too.

But he did win on the president's ineligibility for reelection, which, as we shall discover, turned out to be the most fateful decision of all made by the committee. Here, though, he came to see that he was mistaken, for "once it was decided that the citizens themselves should choose the president, the ill was without remedy, and that any rash attempt to hinder the people in their choice would only increase it." History would soon provide the proof of this particular pudding. "The vote on this matter, and the great influence I had on the result, is my most vexatious memory from that time."

Tocqueville did approve of the committee's work on arrangements for justice under the new republic, which preserved the principle of judges' freedom from dismissal. A court of appeal and a court to judge political crimes were established. Beaumont was the key figure in drafting many of the pertinent clauses here, and Tocqueville thought that the committee's work on justice was likely to be "the only part of the Constitution of 1848 that will survive." As elsewhere in his work on the committee, Tocqueville tried to build in an elasticity that made sensible change possible. In one of his devastating similes, he wrote: "I thought one should treat the French people like those lunatics whom one is careful not to bind lest they become infuriated by the constraint." Despite these small successes, much of the work of the committee was thought, even at the time it was done, provisional; the notion was that later it could be filled out and polished up. This never happened: "The sketch," Tocqueville writes, "was the picture." Yet again practice would make a shambles of theory.

Around the time that the proletariat of Paris had begun to emerge as a force in French politics, Prince Louis-Napoléon, nephew of Napoleon Bonaparte, returned from exile in London to run for—and win—a seat in the Assembly. Conservatives, frightened by the radicals and socialists with their cries of class war, were searching for any and all ways to hold disorder at bay. Louis-Napoléon, through an improbable concatenation of events and personal character, seemed to many the instrument best suited to bring order, not least because he was a Bonaparte, a name that still carried much magic. "I never thought," Tocqueville wrote, "when I heard of Louis-Napoléon's election, that exactly a year later I should be his minister."

After a brief term as president of the republic, General Louis-Eugène Cavaignac, a firm republican who had done much to quell the riots in the streets of Paris, was replaced in that office by Louis-Napoléon. Tocqueville was a supporter of Cavaignac, but when it came time to form his cabinet, Louis-Napoléon, a man who seemed oddly selective in his grudges, decided not to hold one against Tocqueville.

In his own view, Tocqueville was a candidate for ministerial office less because of his politics than, as he himself put it, "because of the great personal consideration I enjoyed outside of politics." By this he meant his prestige as the author of *Democracy in America,* as a member of the Académie Française (to which he had been elected in 1841), and as a man with a reputation for being above traditional party politics. His was, as he wrote, "an honorable position, but one hard to maintain in the midst of parties, and one that would become very precarious if ever the parties turned to violence and consequently became exclusive."

Tocqueville's tendency was to vote with the majority in the Assembly against the socialists and radicals; he, too, held order to be the sine qua non for the conduct of serious politics. He was still hoping to do what he could to help bring the kind of stability to French political life that would permit the steady growth of liberty unimpeded by the regular rumblings of the earthquakes of revolutionary change.

When his name began to be bandied about as a possible cabinet minister, Tocqueville, in his *Recollections,* recalled asking himself, "But ought I to want to be a minister?... I think I can fairly say that I had not the slightest illusions abut the real difficulties of the undertaking, and I saw the future with a clarity one rarely attains except in looking at the past." The situation in the assembly was a steady state—or, more precisely, an unsteady state—with the same old forces contending against one another. He was among the minority of the majority: wanting order, though not at the price of dictatorship; and wanting to retain the republic, though chiefly because he hoped to enlarge liberty under its aegis.

The real question mark, the joker in the deck, was Louis-Napoléon. Tocqueville claimed not really to know him, but what he did know for certain was that Louis-Napoléon wished to rule France. Tocqueville and his political allies were not ready for a return to a monarchy, and especially not under a man with so cloudy a past as Louis-Napoléon's: he was a man with many mistresses, a history of shady dealings, and cronies whom Tocqueville characterized as "intriguers, adventurers, and lackeys." The president and the cabinet he formed, Tocqueville knew, would never be in harmony. "His sympathies were bound always to be elsewhere, for our points of view were not only different but naturally contrary. We wanted to make the republic live; he wished to inherit from it. We offered him no more than ministers when he needed accomplices."

The ministerial post Tocqueville thought himself best fitted for was education. Not only was he a man of considerable learning but he had worked in the Chamber of Deputies for freeing local education and against the centralized curricula set by the universities, and so he knew a fair amount about the various school systems in France. But this post was not to be his. He was instead offered agriculture, which he refused.

In the shuffling of needs, vanities, and little power plays among candidates for ministerial office, Tocqueville drew the card of foreign affairs. This was normally an office of great prestige, but much of its cachet was lost because France, after so many revolutions and counterrevolutions, was not in a position of great power in the world. The problem for a foreign minister, as Tocqueville saw it, was not to let the country's prestige slip further through mistaken entanglements, precipitate actions it could not back up, or retreats from commitments that a great country requires to ensure at least a simulacrum of grandeur. Conciliation much less than aggression, with an ever-watchful eye for the balance of power in Europe, was to provide the general tone of Tocqueville's brief term as minister of foreign affairs.

And brief it was. The term lasted about five months, from June 3 to October 29, 1849. A fine caricature was drawn of Tocqueville at this time by Daumier, over the caption: *Remplaçant M. Douyn de Lhuys. Puisse le lorgnon qu'il tient à la main lui faire voir clair dans les affaires etrangères?* ("Replacing M. Douyn de Lhuys. Can the spectacles that he holds in his hand help him to see clearly into foreign affairs?") In Daumier's rendering, Tocqueville no longer seems the unblemished youth of the often reproduced portrait by Théodore Chassériau that hangs in the National Museum in Versailles. In Daumier's rendering, there is something knowing, if not sly, about Tocqueville's face, much of this conveyed by the mouth, with its thin upper lip, its slightly crooked smile. The eyes are farther apart than normal. The face is lined, the left side darker than the right. The bright young man is gone, replaced by the wily politician and man of affairs.

Tocqueville's tenure as minister of foreign affairs turned out to be more important for him than for France. It lent him the heady feeling of self-mastery. Once on the job, he began by systematically replacing those ambassadors in important places (London, Saint Petersburg, Vienna) for whom he had little regard; he was able, over what he thought might be the objections of Louis-Napoléon, to post Beaumont to Vienna, even though Beaumont had spoken strongly against Louis-Napoléon. Tocqueville also assigned informants in significant countries to fill him in on information not generally available to official ambassadors. He installed the young belletrist Joseph-Arthur de Gobineau as his private secretary, starting that young man on a long diplomatic career.

The handful of problems with which Tocqueville had to deal—in Switzerland, the Middle East, and Algeria; with German unification; but above all in Rome, where French troops had already been sent in to guarantee the return of Pope Pius IX—all show him applying a steady and sophisticated hand, keeping the interest of France always uppermost, and quite properly viewing the world broadly and with cool detachment.

Addressing his ambassadors soon after taking office, Tocqueville said:

> I am no diplomat and I will say my last word at the very start and after that change nothing. I know that France is in no state to dominate Europe and make her wishes prevail in distant lands. Therefore we shall not attempt that. You can count on us leaving you perfectly free in matters beyond our scope, for we shall not worry about making ourselves look important and pretend to

be concurring in such things. But in bordering countries and on questions that affect her directly, France has the right to exercise not just great but preponderant influence. We will not meddle in what happens at the far end of Europe, in the Principalities, in Poland, or in Hungary. But I warn you that you cannot do anything in Belgium, Switzerland, or Piedmont without our advice and concurrence. There we shall not limit ourselves to negotiation but will, if need be, go to war, risking everything to keep our position. I am not trying to hide the fact that a foreign war would be very difficult and dangerous for us at this moment, for our whole social structure might break under the strain, sweeping away our fortunes and our lives. Nevertheless you must realize that, in the case I mentioned, we would even go to war. At least you can be quite certain that I should resign if the President or the Assembly were not ready to follow me so far.

He lived out this policy to the letter. In complex notions over the fate of the Turks, Tocqueville quotes himself writing to his ambassadors in Saint Petersburg and in Vienna: "Handle the business very gently. Be careful not to enlist our adversaries' self-esteem against us. Avoid too great or obvious intimacy with the English ambassadors, whose government is detested at the Courts where you are, while, of course, keeping good relations with those ambassadors. To gain your point, take a friendly tone and do not try to frighten them. Explain our true situation: we do not want war; we hate it; we fear it; but we cannot act dishonorably." The subtleties of diplomacy, as this and several of Tocqueville's other diplomatic communications make clear, were never lost on him.

In his five months in office, Tocqueville scored no thunderous triumphs, but neither did anything go seriously awry on his watch. His reasoning was always complex, his sangfroid never breached. He kept the ball in play, mindful that he was representing a country much torn apart by internal conflict and that "it was a sorry plight to be a minister of Foreign Affairs in such a country at such a time."

When he wrote about his days at the Foreign Ministry in *Recollections,* Tocqueville recorded that, though at first he worried about being daunted by the large responsibilities of the job, in fact they greatly stimulated him. They also provided the occasion for some of his finest introspection. "I felt perplexed, discouraged, and anxious when faced by minor responsibilities. But I felt peculiarly tranquil and calm when faced by great ones." Failure, which had always seemed terrifying to him, was set aside once he was in high office: "The prospect of a crashing fall from my high position in one of the greatest theatres in the world did not trouble me at all, which made me realize that there was much more of pride than of timidity in my constitution." Dealing with difficulties on a daily basis inured him to crises and calmed him generally. He also discovered that power, far from making him more insolent, made him more agreeable, for he "found it much easier to be affable and even cordial when raised above the competition than when I was one of the crowd."

The job also had much to teach him about vanity. Mistaking the man for the job, most people, who had formerly cared little for him, now, he noticed, sought him out, giving great import to his words. Dropping his former hauteur, he discovered that often the most efficacious appeal he could make was to other men's vanity. By bolstering the egos of the powerful—including the ubiquitous Thiers and others whom he "overwhelmed with deference" —he could avoid having to follow their advice. "I found," Tocqueville writes, "that negotiating with men's vanity gives one the best bargain, for one often receives the most substantial advantages in return for very little of substance." And what applied to men often applied to nations: "For nations are like men in that they prefer a fuss made on their behalf to real services rendered."

Even though he had written a book everywhere greeted as a classic in political philosophy, even though he was a man of aristocratic manner and cosmopolitan bearing, Tocqueville remained racked by his great bogey—self-doubt—until his five-month term as minister of French foreign affairs. Summarizing what the job had meant to him, he wrote, "I found myself much less unsuited than I had feared to the task I had undertaken, and that discovery emboldened me, not only for the moment but for the rest of my life. If any one asks me what profit I derived from such an anxious, thwarted, and short period in office, without time to finish anything I had begun, my answer is that I gained one great benefit, perhaps the greatest this world can give, namely confidence in myself."

In the way that life too frequently arranges, just as Tocqueville had gained his full stride as a politician and statesman, his active political life came to an end. For this he had Louis-Napoléon to thank. This strangest of all political figures, whom Tocqueville once described as "a weak and mediocre conqueror," was the man who first promoted and then put paid to Tocqueville's political career. Short, with a large mustache and what many have described as empty eyes, and a penchant for wearing striped military trousers, said to have been the most commonplace and hence boring of speakers, Louis-Napoléon, this most easily caricatured of men, captured the imagination of the French soon after his return from exile. (A rather pathetic attempt at a coup d'état in 1836 resulted in his being deported to America.) After winning his seat in the Assembly, he went on to win the vote for the presidency of the republic by a margin of 4 million votes in a poll of 7 million voters.

The French took to Louis-Napoléon because they hungered for a return to stability combined with a hope for glory of a kind they last knew when his uncle was emperor. The nephew, however dull his utterances, was clever in sedulously cultivating his popularity. He took himself off to every new opening of a railroad line, church function, and provincial ceremonial occasion. Slowly, he accrued a larger and larger following.

Tocqueville was suspicious of Louis-Napoléon's designs from the outset; when the new president asked him to join the cabinet, Tocqueville replied that he would serve him as head of the republic but would never serve him "in overthrowing the republic. But I will gladly strive to assure a great place for you within it." In the same line of reasoning, Tocqueville pledged to himself to "behave each day when a minister as if I would cease to be one on the morrow; that is to say, never to subordinate the need to be myself to that of being a minister." Insofar as it is possible for a politician to remain his own man, Tocqueville appears to have done so.

Of all the ministers serving in Louis-Napoléon's first cabinet, Tocqueville thought himself "most in his good graces," the one who "saw him closest and could judge him best." That Louis-Napoléon thought well of Tocqueville did not mean that so habitually critical a man as Tocqueville was obliged to think well of Louis-Napoléon. Tocqueville's first impressions of him were mixed. In private, Tocqueville found him possessed of "a kindly, easygoing temperament; a human character; a soul that was gentle and even rather tender, but without delicacy; great confidence in his relations with people; a perfect simplicity; an element of personal modesty mixed with immense pride in his ancestry; and a better memory for kindness than for resentment."

On the other side of the ledger, Louis-Napoléon spoke "little and poorly; he had not the art of making others talk and establishing intimacy with them, and no facility in expressing himself.... His powers of dissimulation were considerable; he could be courageous, though also vacillating in his plans"; and his taste for "vulgar enjoyments and comforts increased with the opportunities given by power." His mind was a jumble, "incoherent and confused, being filled with great thoughts ill-clothed," some of them borrowed from his uncle's example, some from socialist theories, and some from memories of England where he had lived for a time. He "firmly believed himself the instrument of destiny and the necessary man," convinced that he shared something akin to the deference owed to the divine line of kings. He had no taste for liberty, and "in political matters the basic characteristic of his mind was hate and contempt for assemblies."

Louis-Napoléon was especially muddled on foreign affairs, which, Tocqueville writes, "showed how ill prepared he was for the role thrust upon him by blind fate." He had no factual knowledge whatsoever, and all he knew was what he was told by others. When Tocqueville instructed him on what ought to be done, he rarely argued, but then refused to act. After a conversation with him on May 15, 1851, Tocqueville noted that Louis-Napoléon had given up on the idea of working well with the Assembly and "is far from renouncing the possibility of a coup d'état on his own account." Finally, Louis-Napoléon kept bad company, even when he no longer needed to do so. And yet, for all this, he was the man for his time: "If Louis-Napoléon had been a wise man, or a genius if you like, he would never have been President of the Republic"—Tocqueville's way of saying that a people gets the leaders it deserves.

Whatever Louis-Napoléon's intellectual deficiencies, for himself, for obtaining his own ends, his actions could scarcely have proved more intelligent. In October 1849, he disbanded his cabinet and selected a new one, this time without appointing a prime minister—an omission which suggested that he would occupy that position himself. He carefully continued to court the people, both Parisians and provincials, in his ceremonial role. Sending troops to protect the pope in Rome brought the church and earnest Catholics over to his side. He identified himself as against the chaos promised by the rebellious socialists, both in the Assembly and in the streets. He began in French politics as Monsieur Bonaparte, soon became known as Louis-Napoléon, and then was often referred to as the "Prince."

Louis-Napoléon relentlessly extended his own powers. The only piece not yet in place for his takeover of power was the army, and this he arranged when he managed to replace as military commander General Changarnier, a staunch defender of the republic, with lesser men then serving in Algeria, whose reputation he inflated. The police were under his control. What forced his hand was that his term as president was up, and this came at a time when he had no inclination whatsoever to return to private life.

The Assembly was faced with either changing the constitution to permit the reelection of a president or opposing Louis-Napoléon outright. It chose the latter, which turned out to be the wrong choice. Although earlier culpable for having insisted on a single presidential term in the constitution, Tocqueville had foreseen problems in Louis-Napoléon's political future. "From the beginning," he wrote in *Recollections*, "I took the line that one must find some *regular* future career for him to prevent him from looking for an irregular one; for it was no use dreaming that he would be President for a time and nothing more."

On the morning of December 2, 1851, Louis-Napoléon set in motion his coup d'état. Posters all over Paris appeared announcing the dissolution of the Assembly and proclaiming a new government. Thiers and other deputies who had ruled France from behind the scenes were awakened by the police and taken off to prison. Cavaignac, Changarnier, and other generals loyal to the republic were detained under arms. Soldiers rode through the streets crying out *Vive l'empereur!* and *Aux Tuileries!* (the Tuileries being the traditional Parisian residence of French kings).

A scattering of some 230 deputies, Tocqueville among them, met at the Assembly to declare everything Louis-Napoléon had done illegal; but, finding their entry blocked, they repaired to the *mairie* of the tenth *arrondissement,* where they officially decreed the coup d'état against the law. It was so much spitting in the wind. Ill at the time, Tocqueville lay down on a coat in a corner, his eyes closed, as bad history washed over him. The military arrived under the command of General Élie-Frédéric Forey, and the dissenting deputies were marched off to the barracks of the Quai d'Orsay; Tocqueville was in a contingent of fifty deputies later shifted to Vincennes, where they remained until December 4. At some risk, Tocqueville wrote a letter to the London *Times* recounting in precise detail the abuses of liberty that had taken place in France and calling on England "as the grand jury of mankind in the cause of freedom" to make the correct judgment of the oppressive nature of the coup d'état. All to no effect.

To much greater personal effect, Louis-Napoléon's coup

d'état meant the end of Tocqueville's active political life. The new emperor later put out feelers suggesting that Tocqueville's services to his government would be welcome should he wish to return; but Tocqueville could never bring himself to serve a man he considered a usurper and despot. He had fought as best he could for the political liberty in which he so ardently believed—had given it, in all, thirteen years of his life—without any result, except self-education. He would spend the days remaining to him fighting the same fight, but conducting it now from libraries, archives, and his own desk.

Chapter Ten

IN 1850, BECAUSE of a serious breakdown in his health— a pulmonary attack that caused him, for the first time, to bring up blood when he coughed—Tocqueville repaired with his wife to the gentler climate of Sorrento. From there, in September, sensing his days as a political figure ending and perhaps even feeling his life drawing to a close, he wrote to his old friend Louis de Kergorlay: "It seems to me that my true worth is above all works of the mind; that I am worth more in thought than in action; and that, if there remains anything of me in this world, it will be much more the trace of what I have written than the recollection of what I will have done. The last ten years, which have been rather sterile for me in many respects, have nonetheless given me the truest insights into human affairs and a more practical sense of the details." Such claims as he had on posterity, in other words, were likely to derive from his intellectual rather than his political activities.

To a true writer, which Tocqueville most assuredly was, nothing is ever wasted, not even more than a decade of empty debate and pointless politicking carried out in public to no obviously useful end. After the coup d'état of 1851, writing was what was left to Tocqueville. But the question was what to write. His first idea was a work centered on Napoleon Bonaparte. This was not to be; it was one of those books that Balzac called "enchanted cigarettes," by which he meant books writers dream about yet never get around to writing, like Tolstoy's begun but unfinished novel on the Decembrists. What a book on Napoleon Tocqueville might have made! Alas, it remains part of that small, rich, and highly select library of great books never written.

Part of the reason that Tocqueville could not have sustained interest in a book on Napoleon was that his primary concern was neither biography nor even history in isolation. The past mattered to him chiefly as it impinged—as impinge it inevitably did—on the present and future. "Basically, only things of our time interest the public and really interest me," he wrote. "The greatness and uniqueness of the spectacle presented by our contemporary world absorb too much of our attention for us to attach much importance to those historical curiosities which are enough for learned and leisured societies." The past was useful as a way to understand how we got where we are now. This sounds shallowly utilitarian, yet one wonders if it wasn't his very present-mindedness that makes Tocqueville so readable in our own day.

Tocqueville viewed French society as undergoing a continuous revolution—a revolution that had thus far lasted more than sixty years and whose end was neither in sight nor to be predicted. Always an adroit metaphor-maker, Tocqueville pictured himself, and the French nation with him, as lost at sea in a boat, in a storm that showed no signs of ever letting up. "I find myself without a compass, without sails or rudder on a sea whose shores I cannot see," he wrote to a friend, "and, weary of useless activity, I lie down at the bottom of the boat and await the future." In *Recollections*, using this same metaphor, he wrote: "I am tired of mistaking deceptive mists for the bank. And I often wonder whether that solid land that we have sought for so long actually exists, and whether it is not our fate to rove the seas for ever." The note of despair is familiar in Tocqueville. In the end, though, he never let his despair, if one may so put it, get him down—not really, not finally. He wrote his way out of it. If he could find the appropriate book to write, perhaps now, too, all would be well.

Still, the question remained: what book ought he to write? As Tocqueville explained to Louis de Kergorlay, he could undertake to write only a book that "animates me and draws out of me all that I can give. I am the man least fit in the world for going up with any advantage against the current of my mind and my taste, and I fall well below mediocre when I do not take an impassioned pleasure in what I am doing."

Tocqueville was also hoping to find a subject for a book that would please the educated public, as *Democracy in America* had done—the sweet smell of its success must never have left his mind. Whatever he wrote, he would fall back on his old method of "judging facts rather than recounting them"; "to tell and to judge at the same time" had become his manner and his mark. Narrative was not his specialty; analysis was. Style, but accessible style, was required to bring off a book of the kind he wanted to write: "Make a strong effort," he wrote in a note to himself, "to avoid as much as possible ... the abstract style, in order to make myself fully understood and, above all, read with pleasure. Make a constant effort to contain abstract and general ideas in words which present a precise and particular picture.... One writes in order to please, and not to attain an ideal perfection of language."

Finally, the book Tocqueville set to work on, *The Old Regime and the Revolution,* was an attempt to discover not only the causes of the French Revolution but why revolution had broken out in such a spectacular way in France, and why at the close of the eighteenth century. In a note to himself about the planned second volume on the revolution, which he did not live long enough to complete, Tocqueville wrote: "My subject was to find the causes of the old regime's death. This naturally led me to study in particular its ills, from which it came about that, without wanting to, I have created something that resembles a diatribe against it."

The book that Tocqueville eventually wrote was part of his continuing campaign—part explanation, part exhortation—to save his country from the danger that democracy, uncontrolled, presented of leading from ochlocracy (or mob rule) on to despotism. It is important to recall that while he was thinking about this book, he felt that a true (if rather pathetic) despot,

Louis-Napoléon, was holding France in thrall. He hoped to save the French by explaining to them how they got to the state they were in, and then providing a map to show how they might escape from it.

The book would be "a mixture of history properly so called with historical philosophy." The first would "supply the canvas and the second the color." Worry though he might about commanding the intellect and art required for such a task, he also believed himself "better suited than anyone else to bring to such a subject great freedom of mind, and to speak without passion and without reticence concerning men and things. For, as regards to men, although they have lived in our time, I am sure I do not hold toward them either love or hate; and as regards to the forms of what are called constitutions, laws, dynasties, classes, they have, so to speak, I will not say no value, but no existence in my eyes, independently of the effects they produce. I have no traditions, I have no party, I have no *cause*, if it is not that of liberty and human dignity; of that, I am sure."

A work of genuine scholarship is not what Tocqueville had in mind when he began *The Old Regime and the Revolution*, but that is what, almost against his wishes, he turns out to have written. To make his point, and to prove his general argument, he needed to search archives both in Paris and in such cities as Tours and in the provinces. What he was after was a picture of how government in France worked, in its minute mechanics and larger policy, before the French Revolution toppled what people long before began to refer to as the *ancien régime*. As part of his preparation, he betook himself and Mme. Tocqueville to

Bonn for several months to study political conditions in feudal Germany. To understand the French Revolution itself, he needed to know, with some precision and in detail, the conditions that had brought it about and why revolution did not occur in other countries at the same time.

If Tocqueville wrote *Democracy in America* with his eye on France, he wrote portions of *The Old Regime and the Revolution* with the United States at the back of his mind. To begin with, there was the distinctive difference between American and French history. The American Revolution was of course something of a misnomer: it was not truly a revolution at all but mainly an extended act of rebellion against what had come to seem an unfair occupying power. Far from pitting class against class, attempting radically to alter power arrangements within the country, struggling to do away with old injustices, and punishing the perpetrators severely, the Americans wished chiefly to shake free of British control. The Americans didn't have a history to rewrite. Setting out very nearly as a tabula rasa, they charged themselves not with changing an existing society so much as with making an entirely new one. If *Democracy in America* is a how-to book on living with the new equality, *The Old Regime and the Revolution* comes closer to being a how-not-to book on the same subject.

Tocqueville saw that American mores formed the politics of the American nation, whereas in France politics tended to form the nation's mores. As François Furet, one of the most penetrating of modern French historians, put it, "In the first case, history has subordinated the state to society; in the second, it has handed society over to the state." To their revolution, more-over, the French brought a vast historical valise, filled with long overdue bills of complaints, grievances, and resentments against a hated aristocracy and a moribund monarchy, made on behalf of a landowning peasantry and an urban proletariat, both with a strong set of ever-rising expectations. Conditions were much closer to feudalism in Germany at the end of the eighteenth century, yet no revolution had broken out there. The English had a more confident and active aristocracy, yet sustained violent revolution in England was never a serious possibility. Why in France and why toward the close of the eighteenth century did the greatest revolution of modernity—greater in its ultimate ramifications, surely, than the Bolshevik revolution of 1917—find its most fertile ground?

Although Alexis de Tocqueville's life was shadowed, indeed haunted, by the French Revolution, he never lost sight of its original attraction and never slighted the grand impulses behind it. As he remarks in the preface to *The Old Regime and the Revolution*, those who made the French Revolution "wanted to create not only democratic institutions but free ones; they sought not only to destroy privileges but to honor and recognize rights. It was a time of youth, enthusiasm, pride, a time of generous and sincere emotions [shades of the young Wordsworth], whose memory, despite its mistakes, will always be preserved by humanity, and which, for a long time to come, will trouble the sleep of all those who wish to corrupt or enslave France."

Tocqueville had become a connoisseur of revolution and of revolutionaries. "A revolution," he wrote, "can sometimes be just and necessary; it can establish liberty; but the *esprit révo-lutionnaire* is always detestable and can never lead anywhere except to tyranny." Elsewhere he wrote that he did not think "there is in France a man less revolutionary than I, nor one who has a more profound hatred for what is called the revolution-ary spirit." This is so because, among other reasons, "all great revolutions ... make people misunderstand what they can do, deceiving in turn both their enemies and their friends." Much of what he has to say on the subject of revolution also has im-pressive prophetic weight. Consider the following in the light of the Russian revolution and the rise of Joseph Stalin: "What must be further noted is that at the beginning of revolutions of this kind, the greatest men can do nothing, and that on the contrary at the end a mediocre man can do everything, if cir-cumstances favor him."

The beginning of Tocqueville's quest in *The Old Regime and the Revolution* was to discover how the grandeur at the heart of the French Revolution slipped away into the alternating des-potism and bumbling regimes which followed it and to which, in his lifetime, no end seemed in sight. "I will try to show what events, what errors and miscalculations, made those same French abandon their original course and, forgetting liberty, desire nothing more than to become the equal servants of the master of the world. I will show how a stronger government, much more absolute than that which the Revolution had over-thrown, arose and concentrated all power in itself, suppressed all the freedoms so dearly bought, and put vain idols in their place." Or, as he put it later in the book, "Never was such a great event, with such ancient causes, so well prepared and so little foreseen."

In *The Old Regime and the Revolution,* Tocqueville shows how this came about. As always, the standard of excellence for him is liberty. The good society is the free society, the one that gives the widest latitude within reason to liberty, for only liberty "can effectively combat the natural vices of these kinds of societies and prevent them from sliding down the slippery slope where they find themselves. Only freedom can bring citizens out of the isolation in which the very independence of their circumstances has led them to live, can daily force them to mingle, to join together through the need to communicate with one another, persuade each other, and satisfy each other in the conduct of their common affairs.... Only freedom can substitute higher and stronger passions for the love of material well-being, give rise to greater ambitions than the acquisition of a fortune, and create the atmosphere which allows one to see and judge human vices and virtues."

What Tocqueville discovered in his various researches was that, from the time of Louis XIV, government in France had become more and more centralized. Through this centralization the old aristocracy had slowly ceded its responsibilities while clinging to its privileges, along the way making itself odious because otiose, living off the fat of the land without contributing anything in return. Local *parlements,* once a force in the French provinces, began to lose their power and hence their function. Central government took over the justice system. Taxes were collected centrally, under the authority of the Minstry of the Interior, and fell most heavily on the peasantry, as did the custom of the corvée, or assignment of labor without wages for working on the building and upkeep of roads. Military service, too, fell most heavily on the poor. Under these arrangements, bureaucracy became the new aristocracy. "If centralization did not perish in the Revolution," Tocqueville wrote, "it was because centralization itself was the beginning of the Revolution and its sign."

"It was not tyranny but paternalism that made us what we are"—here was one of Tocqueville's major discoveries. First from Versailles (home of the Sun King) and then from Paris, all power and succor flowed. Big Brother was not so much watching as helping every step of the way. Not that centralization was ever perfected—"the old regime in a nutshell," Tocqueville noted, was "a rigid rule, lax implementation"—but it was pervasive. How pervasive he learned through studying the documents of the time. Among the most useful were those of the *intendants,* as the chief bureaucratic officers of the old regime were called, who had much in common with the bureaucrats of his own day. "If you have read a prefect," he writes, "you have read an *intendant.*"

But Tocqueville, being Tocqueville, knew that laws and institutions alone were not sufficient either to explain or to move a people, even though he allowed that "the slow and constant action of institutions" can sometimes be more decisive than monarchs and powerful men. "I am quite convinced," he wrote to his lawyer and friend Pierre Freslon, echoing his old refrain, "that political societies are not what their laws make them, but what sentiments, beliefs, ideas, habits of the heart, and the spirit of the men who form them, prepare them in advance to be, as well as what nature and education have made them."

France of the eighteenth century is customarily treated as the Age of Enlightenment. Tocqueville was perhaps the period's first revisionist: he saw the philosophes, as the scientists and intellectuals of the age are often called, doing as much as anyone to help abrogate liberty. Through their writings they changed sentiments, beliefs, and habits, all in the name of a "reason" that, in Tocqueville's view, had very little to do with actual experience.

He deals with the influence of Voltaire and the great figures of the French Enlightenment in a chapter titled "How Around the Middle of the Eighteenth Century Intellectuals Became the Country's Leading Politicians, and the Effects Which Resulted from This." Not all are mentioned by name, but the cast of players—philosophers, scientists, men of letters—is well enough known: Diderot, d'Alembert, Rousseau, D'Holbach, Helvétius, Condillac, the physiocrats, and the rest. Recognizing that there were serious differences among these figures, Tocqueville nonetheless thought them united behind, and energized by, a single overpowering idea: "They all think that it would be good to substitute basic and simple principles, derived from reason and natural law, for the complicated and traditional customs which ruled the society of their times." Chief among these simple principles were that reason (understood as pure ratiocination) is more efficient than custom and tradition, and that few things were less reasonable than religion.

The philosophes began from the absurd arrangements of the society into which they had been born: the unearned privileges of the aristocrats on the one hand and the unreasonable burdens placed on the common people on the other. They themselves had no palpable power, and not even secondhand experience of power. They flew, so to say, on pure love of abstract theory and hatred of tradition. They were further blinded by not having lived with true liberty, having grown up bound by the centralized government favored by the century's monarchs. "At the almost infinite distance from practice in which they lived, no experience tempered the ardors of their nature," Tocqueville wrote, "nothing warned them of the obstacles that existing facts might place before even the most desirable reforms; they didn't have any idea of the dangers which always accompany even the most necessary revolutions."

Tocqueville goes on to describe how, in the absence of either a genuinely active and useful aristocracy or vibrant local politics, the people of France were entranced by the theoretical speculations of the philosophes. Such theorizing soon came to resemble a parlor game, which anyone who had a political grievance, a sense of somewhere or somehow being unjustly treated by laws and institutions, could play. The main idea of the philosophes, on which many variations were set out, was the necessity for equality of all ranks. And who, except for the already debased aristocrats, wouldn't officially approve of that?

A general belief in the power of education also rendered France susceptible to seduction by the theoretical-minded philosophes, making it possible for a great nation to be "completely shaped by men of letters." Behind the programs of the philosophes was the idea that education itself would redeem all, including men's and women's souls, though they wouldn't have used the words "redeem" or "souls." (Tocqueville wrote to an American clergyman, Louis Dwight: "There are people in France who have a blind love for instruction. They believe that simply by having taught a man to read, write, and count, one has made of him a good citizen and almost a virtuous man.") In our own day, of course, this notion of the redemptive power of education retains great currency: enough education will root out evil, stimulate goodness, show the way, making life better for one and all. Educate, educate, educate—and sweetness and light will follow.

Tocqueville also adduces the strong impression that the leading figures of the American revolution, many of them philosophes in their own way, made on the French, who followed events in the United States very closely. "The Americans seemed merely to apply what our writers had thought of: they gave substantial reality to what we were dreaming about." What the French philosophes didn't have, of course, was the fresh start that Providence had granted the American founding fathers.

The philosophes brought, as Tocqueville remarks, "all the habits of literature into politics. The problem is that "what is merit in a writer is sometimes vice in a statesman, and the same things which have often made lovely books can lead to great revolutions." Such was their prominence that even unlettered peasants began to use the language of the philosophes. "To become mediocre men of letters, all they had to do was learn how to spell." Tocqueville closes his chapter on the intellectuals and revolutionary politics by reminding his readers that the vaporous ideas of so many of these men have remained alive in his own day, a hundred years later, even in the minds of those who despise writers and have read little literature—as, of course, they remain alive today.

The influence of the literary mind resulted in "unlimited confidence in reason and the government's actions." Tocqueville claimed this to be not merely an idea of the eighteenth century but one peculiar to France, "born of inexperience and the sight of absolute government. Faith in reason has been extinguished by experience, but the idea of government as creator and safety net has remained." To faith in reason was added the French believe in equality. "Everyday experience," Tocqueville's cousin Chateaubriand wrote, "proves that the French turn instinctively toward power: they have no love at all for liberty; equality alone is their idol."

The same philosophes who staked all on reason also attacked religion. In their minds religion was the great anti-reason. Religion was nowhere without its antagonists, but only in France, Tocqueville claimed, had irreligion become a general passion, ardently preached by Voltaire and others and taken up by large segments of the population. Elsewhere, established religions had been attacked on behalf of newer or emerging religions. But in France Christianity was attacked without any attempt to put another religion in its place. "Absolute unbelief in matters of religion, which is so contrary to the natural instincts of humanity and puts its soul into such a painful position, seemed attractive to the crowd." There were voices of unbelief in Germany, England, and even America, but only in France did they resound so sonorously; only in France was "impiety ... the pastime of idle lives." Reason, not God, was to be venerated.

Tocqueville's explanation for this is to blame not the church, which in France was no more retrograde than elsewhere, but the philosophes, who, as he put it, felt that "in order to attack the institutions of the state, it was necessary to destroy those of the church, which served as foundation and model for them." The reason for this was that monarchs gave the church its temporal power, and the church lent the monarchs their moral sanction. For the philosophes, the pleasure of doing so was redoubled because it was the church that chiefly censored writers and intellectuals.

"Without doubt," Tocqueville writes, "the universal discredit into which all religious beliefs fell at the end of the last century exercised the greatest influence on the whole of our Revolution; it marked its character. Nothing did more to give its features that terrible expression which we have seen." As he had noted in *Democracy in America,* "despotism can do without faith, but liberty cannot"—and that comment includes, of course, the despotism of the majority.

The result of the cumulative attack on the church in France was that political religion filled the place left by actual religion. Perfection, which Christianity makes plain is not available in this life, under the religion of politics becomes a possibility. The French Revolution, Tocqueville wrote, "became a new kind of religion, an incomplete religion, it is true, without God, without ritual, and without a life after death, but one which nevertheless, like Islam, flooded the earth with its soldiers, apostles, and martyrs." Under this new religion without God, men had only themselves to fall back on, and fall back on themselves they did; under the new dispensation, the state, not God, would make man. In other words, left to themselves, with only the appetite for equality and the concomitant destruction of all rank, men lost their anchor, their balance, their orientation. Formerly, religion acted as an obstacle to unbounded perfectionism. Marx may have been right in saying that religion was the opiate of the people. But the religion of politics can provide an even stronger, more dangerous drug. It could be as murderous as traditional religion, as witness the Terror; it could be still more murderous, as witness the Nazis and Soviet and Chinese communism. But for Tocqueville, the immediate result of the ascendancy of the religion of politics was the loss of love for liberty.

Tocqueville everywhere states his own love for liberty, in whose defense he claims—and there is no reason to doubt him—to be prepared to give his life. "I regard liberty as the prime good," he writes to Madame Swetchine, in a characteristic utterance, "as I have always seen in it one of the most fertile sources of manly virtue and of great actions. Neither tranquillity nor well-being can take its place." But, as mentioned earlier, he does not, in any detail, describe the value of liberty, nor does he precisely attempt to demonstrate its effects. ("Of all the loose Terms in the world," Edmund Burke wrote, "Liberty is the most indefinite.") But for Tocqueville liberty at a minimum would allow room for independent thought, high ambition, devotion to great causes. "Do not ask me to describe this sublime desire [for liberty]," he wrote; "it must be felt. It enters of itself into great hearts that God has prepared to receive it; it fills them, it fires them. One must give up making this comprehensible to the mediocre souls who have never felt it." He may at times have been ambivalent about religion, but about liberty never.

How both liberty and religion operated in Tocqueville's thought are seen to good advantage in his correspondence with Arthur Gobineau, the young man whom he had hired as his secretary when he was minister of foreign affairs and with whom he kept in touch until his own death. Gobineau went on to a fairly distinguished career in diplomacy, holding ambassadorships in Bern, Frankfurt, Tehran, Athens, and elsewhere. Gobineau had great regard for Tocqueville, writing to his family that "it is impossible to even imagine a more profoundly good and affectionate man," while Tocqueville had perhaps less regard but nonetheless always a kindly feeling for Gobineau.

Gobineau was a Germanophile, and an ardent admirer of the Nordic races generally. Ranking the races was his obsession, and, as Tocqueville early tried to demonstrate to him, a source of profound intellectual error. Gobineau made the error public when he published his *Essai sur l'inégalité des races humaine*. In their exchange of letters on this subject, Tocqueville says that he can never believe in Gobineau's ideas about racial ranking: first because they violate his Christian beliefs and second because they are an affront to his belief in the importance of liberty.

In one of these letters, Tocqueville suggests that Gobineau's "scientific [read racial] theories" are not easily reconciled "with the letter and even the spirit of Christianity." Christianity, after all, posits all men as related, at once brothers and equals. "Your doctrine makes of them cousins at most." Gobineau's views also make education, reform, and improvement impossible for those races he had ranked low "as a consequence of a certain original disposition which cannot change and which irresistibly limits the perfecting of some."

What Tocqueville detests about Gobineau's theories is their determinism. For Gobineau all the cards are dealt, with no more to be drawn. What possible use, Tocqueville wonders, could such a theory be to humanity? "Do you not see that your doctrine brings out naturally all the evils that permanent inequality creates—pride, violence, the contempt of fellow men, tyranny, and abjectness under all its forms?"

Behind Gobineau's theories, Tocqueville finds a low view of human possibility—a view that he does not share. These racist views have caused Gobineau to lose any feeling for the fight against despotism, and instead to view men as big children awaiting a master. Tocqueville could not disagree more strongly. He continues to hold out hope, thinking that "human societies like individuals become something only through the practice of liberty.... No, I will not believe that this human species, which is at the head of visible creation, should become the debased flock that you tell us it is and that there is nothing more to do than to deliver it without future and without recourse to a small number of shepherds who, after all, are not better animals than we are and often are worse. You will permit me to have more confidence than you in the bounty and justice of God." Reading this, one wants to rise from one's chair and applaud.

In the midst of this attack, Tocqueville offers the assurance that he intends to do what he can to help Gobineau attain membership in the Academy of Moral and Political Sciences. Tocqueville had a talent for friendship, and it seemed to become greater as he grew older. Certain of his friends—Beaumont, Kergorlay, Jean-Jacques Ampère, Corcelle—he kept for decades, and there is good reason to believe that they loved him. For a man one thinks of as icy in temperament and reticent by nature, Tocqueville could be quite confessional with his dearest friends, not hesitating to fill them in on his doubts, his discouragements, his all-too-human needs.

So to Madame Swetchine he writes, in connection with his worries about the reception of the first volume of *The Old Regime and the Revolution,* "I would very much like to have the virtue of being indifferent to success, but I do not possess it." He writes to Beaumont that he cannot bear to think about his manuscript, so certain is he that it is poor stuff, "this unhappy manuscript [that] burns my fingers and suggests to me, as I go over it, the most disagreeable sensations (the word is well chosen, because it is a matter of a kind of physical horror). To that anxiety is joined the anxiety that the future of a book always causes even those who see themselves in a good light."

When he turns to the second volume of this work, he allows, to Kergorlay, that he is drowning in the vast sea of research material. He knows the right questions; he knows what he is looking for; "but try as I may I cannot raise the veil that covers it. I feel this object as if through a strange body, preventing me from either touching it well or seeing it." To Beaumont he writes that "I am lost in an ocean of research and in the midst of it I am sometimes overcome by fatigue and discouragement." He felt that he was writing a book which would please no one and in which no one could possibly be interested. If *Democracy in America* had been meant as the equivalent of Montesquieu's *Spirit of the Laws*, *The Old Regime and the Revolution* was to parallel Montesquieu's *Considerations on the Causes of the Greatness of the Romans and Their Decline*. But, Tocqueville was now certain, it was not to be.

The first volume of the book Tocqueville so worried about was published, in 1856, to much praise, both in France and in England, where his friend Henry Reeve had done a translation. Some readers did not understand the subtlety of Tocqueville's argument in this book; others were too committed to their own politics to be able to accept it. But such criticism as the book received, from the usual suspects, was not sufficient to stop it from going into four editions or from changing the view of the origins of the French Revolution forevermore.

In his preface to this first volume, Tocqueville sketched out his ambitious plan for the full book, which was to describe the background to the revolution, proceed to the work of the revolution itself, and then move on to investigate the effects on the new society to which the revolution had given birth. "Will I be able to finish it?" he asked. "Who can say? The fate of individuals is still more hidden than that of nations." Of his second volume, he completed only two chapters, did rough drafts of seven others, and left sheaves of tantalizing notes from his researches and instructions to himself. But the account of the actual French Revolution and all that followed was never written, and the work in the end has to be considered incomplete and, as it were, half a classic. The full version of *The Old Regime and the Revolution* remains another enchanted cigarette.

Chapter Eleven

O N   A N   A U G U S T   afternoon in Cherbourg in 1850, out for
a walk with his friends Nassau Senior and Jean-Charles
Rivet, the forty-five-year-old Alexis de Tocqueville, in a reminiscent mood, remarked to his friends on his envy of his ser-
vant Eugène. "If happiness consists in the correspondence of
our wishes to our powers, as I believe it does," he said, "he must
be happy." As for himself, he allows that "all my life been striv-
ing at things not one of which I shall completely obtain." Nine
years later, when Tocqueville was on his deathbed, it seems
doubtful that he would have revised that statement. He died,
there is good reason to think, believing his life considerably less
than a success.

Although he had served several terms in his country's various legislative, constituent, and national assemblies and had
briefly achieved the key post of minister of foreign affairs, as
an active politician and statesman he felt himself a fizzle. "In

French politics," François Furet has justly written, "Tocqueville never had his moment."

Democracy in America was a genuine accomplishment, all the more remarkable for having been written when its author was so young; yet it is far from clear that this book and all the praise and fame it garnered for its author were laurels on which Tocqueville could find any rest. He intended the book, after all, in part as a launch for even greater things. About *The Old Regime and the Revolution* he must have felt the heavy weight of incompletion, and hence ultimately of defeat. His *Recollections*, splendid of their kind, were, by his instruction, not to be published in his lifetime, so he had no public authentication of his achievement in this book. He had a solid enough marriage, but left no children—another source of sadness in his life.

So often do doubt and despair come up in Tocqueville's correspondence that one has to wonder if he might have been a depressive, in the spiritual if not the strictly clinical sense, for about the latter we cannot of course know. Perhaps he was instead someone whose superior perspective left him naturally disappointed with his life. F. Scott Fitzgerald says that it is natural for an intelligent man in middle age to be mildly depressed: his youth is over; his mistakes cannot be undone; the room to maneuver and elude what begins to look like his fate is greatly lessened; death is closing in.

But the melancholy strain in Tocqueville was there almost from the outset. Sainte-Beuve wrote that Tocqueville's sadness was comparable to that of "Aeneas setting out to found the city of Rome, though still weeping for Dido." Tocqueville had to a very high power what Henry James called—and James himself also had it—the "imagination of disaster," or the ability always to see the worst possible outcome. So, for Tocqueville, democracy, whatever its virtues, was always in danger of lapsing into tyranny. "Why," he asked in his notebooks from America, "as civilizations spread, do outstanding men become fewer? Why, when attainments are the lot of all, do great intellectual talents become rarer? Why, when there are no longer lower classes, are there no more upper classes?"

Twenty-two years later, in the midst of composing *The Old Regime and the Revolution,* he wrote, "One predicts that no intellectual greatness will be left [in France] except among people who protest against the government of their country and who remain free amid servitude. If there appear here some great minds, this will not be because anything great is happening in the country; but because there will be found some souls who will retain the imprint of better times." Tocqueville was a man who, shown a silver lining, could always locate the cloud.

He was also a man who spent much time on that saddest of all themes: what might have been—especially what might have been in his own life and career. He blamed some of what he construed to be his failure on the political life of his times. As early as 1833, he wrote to Eugène Stoffels: "I struggle with all my power against this bastard wisdom, this fatal indifference which in our times is sapping the energy of so many beautiful souls. I try not to make two worlds: the one moral, where I still get excited about what is beautiful and good; the other political, where to smell more comfortably the dung on which we walk, I stretch out flat on my stomach." But he committed, as we know, so many years of his life to the latter world, the political—and with so little gain, as he knew.

He seemed no less dubious of his undoubted intellectual abilities. Writing to Royer-Collard about the final chapter of *Democracy in America,* he remarks, "The substance gives me plenty of other concerns: I sense that I am treating there the most important idea of our time; its grandeur raises me up, but my own inadequacy weighs me down. I catch sight of all that could be said concerning such a subject, and I know that it is not I who will say it." He did say it, of course, in many ways and from many angles, better than anyone else before or since, but it was somehow not in his nature to believe completely in his own powers.

His dolor weighed heavily on him, even when he was young and his life full of promise. Reporting the crowdedness of his and Beaumont's days in Boston, he wrote to Madame de Grancey: "Besides, you know that the great object in life is to forget, as soon as it is possible, that one exists." From Washington, at the end of his tour of America, he wrote to his brother Édouard: "I did not suppose that I could possibly return to my country with so much darkness in my soul." Eight years later, to Édouard again, he writes that "what moves the soul is different, but the soul is the same—this anxious and insatiable soul that despises all the good things of the world and which, nonetheless, incessantly needs to be stirred in order to seize them, so as to escape the grievous numbness that it experiences as soon as it relies for a moment on itself. This is a sad story. It is a little bit the story of all men, but of some more than others, and of myself more than anyone I know."

Such was the depth of Tocqueville's self-doubt that it went beyond a melancholy nature to take on an almost neurotic coloring. George Wilson Pierson picks up on this in various places in his *Tocqueville in America*. "By nature," he writes, "Tocqueville had such a horror of any kind of uncertainty, that one is almost tempted to see in this dialectic [his method of playing the inductive and deductive off each other] primarily an elaborate mechanism of doubt." His perfectionism issued out of the same source. "For himself," Pierson writes, "he was incapable of letting a thing go until persuaded he 'could not do better.' By personal taste and by a sort of nervous compulsion, both, he invited the torture of perfection." In America, he reads documents composed in George Washington's hand and compares it—unfavorably, naturally—with his own impatient, nervous scrawl. Tocqueville preferred not to pass up an opportunity to put himself down.

Again, though he sent off his manuscripts to his family and select friends, Tocqueville often had a problem making use of the help of others. "He had to think things through for himself," Pierson notes, "and he wanted no disturbing guidance. In fact, so delicate was the balance of his nerves that an outside suggestion before he had made up his own mind—or a contradictory opinion expressed after his mind was made up—would often upset him, throw all his meditations awry, and make him desperately unhappy for days."

What an astonishing amalgam of the contrarieties Alexis

de Tocqueville presented: highly ambitious yet deeply pessimistic, arrogant yet insecure, courageous yet dubious, bold yet anxious, highly moral yet often with a low view of the motives of men, thoughtful yet without much gift for repose, forever seeking for truth yet knowing it wasn't available to mere men. ("I finally convinced myself," he wrote to Charles Stoffels, "that the search for absolute, *demonstrable* truth, like the search for perfect happiness, was an effort after the impossible.") From the outside, he appeared to have everything that makes for the calm enjoyment of life; on the inside, he underwent much more than the normal turmoil of worry and doubt.

Why? Why did this man who, apart from his poor health, was otherwise seemingly so well set up to enjoy life find it so great a struggle? Why did sustained tranquillity elude him? The best method for finding a measure of contentment was, as he once said, "to be able to set your mind to work on theoretical subjects." Why theoretical? Perhaps because the cast of his mind tended that way: Beaumont reported that "Alexis de Tocqueville did not have a memory for words or numbers, but to the highest degree he possessed a memory for ideas; once entered into his mind, an idea never escaped." Tocqueville's own view was that, "whatever anyone says, it is ideas that stir the world, not blind needs." And yet, as we have seen, he was also distrustful of ideas.

He was himself a man who had one idea. This idea was that equality was relentlessly, inevitably, and irreversibly sweeping the world. The idea was not wholly original, but in his hands it was extremely fruitful, and it proliferated into many other ideas. Unlike Marx, Malthus, or Freud, Tocqueville was not, in Wallace Stevens's phrase, a "lunatic of one idea." His idea led its possessor to sociological considerations, to historical insights, to philosophical observations, to pondering and puzzling out as best he was able that greatest of all riddles, how human nature (itself an unsolvable mystery) responds in the crucible of historical experience.

Every idea, it has been said, has its origin in autobiography. What led Tocqueville to the idea of the spread of equality and its consequences is not difficult to understand. He had a personal stake in equality—at the outset, one might say, in inequality. The arrival of equality led to the departure of the aristocracy into which, too late, he was born. Under a flourishing aristocracy, how different, potentially how much more glorious, his life might have been. Tocqueville never claimed to love democracy; he claimed only to recognize its inevitability and permanence, and to discover what might best be made of it; he also recognized that aristocracy had done itself in and could never be resuscitated. He wrote to reassure a reviewer of *The Old Regime and the Revolution*, who claimed that he, Tocqueville, advocated a return to aristocracy, that "I am a sincere and ardent friend of what you yourself consider the main conquests of the Revolution: political liberty and all the individual liberties that this expression contains, the abolition of all caste privileges, equality before the law, total religious liberty, simple legislation." But from the second volume of *Democracy in America* a threnody could be composed over Tocqueville's regret about the death of aristocracy. Under aristocracy, for all that it was often tyrannical, even inhuman, souls are nonetheless raised to a higher pitch, and "vast ideas of dignity, power, and grandeur of man are widely entertained." Under aristocracy, science is cultivated for its truth and beauty, without being weighed down by practical necessity, and this "cannot be the same in democratic nations." Under aristocracy, artisans, working to satisfy the few, produce with an eye to perfection such as will satisfy those with the highest standards; under aristocracy, "the aim of the arts is to do the best possible work, not the quickest or the cheapest." So it is that "aristocracies produce a small number of great paintings, whereas democratic countries produce a multitude of minor ones. The former raise statues of bronze; the latter make plaster casts." As with the visual arts, so with the literature. "In aristocratic nations, certain privileged individuals enjoy an existence that is in a sense outside the human condition, and above it. Among their seemingly exclusive prerogatives are power, wealth, glory, wit, delicacy, and distinction of every sort." This is the life Tocqueville, by being born too late, missed.

But Tocqueville's problem went deeper. In good part, it may have been a religious problem. Doubt began when he lost his secure hold on religious belief. In his writings, he invoked God and Providence with an ease that a contemporary writer would find difficult to manage, and in a manner that goes well beyond mere rhetorical ornament. He told his beloved teacher Abbé Lesueur that he still believed in what his religion taught, but could no longer practice it. A strong case can be made that, the closer to death he grew, the more he longed for belief of the kind that made practice possible.

Certainly, in his writings he was a great friend to religion. The Catholic historian Christopher Dawson held that Tocqueville was a greater historian than Thiers or Guizot, owing "to the breadth of his spiritual vision and to the strength of his religious faith." Tocqueville linked religion with liberty, believed the former a necessary encouragement to the latter, and believed further that the philosophes may have struck their most powerful blow for revolution and against order and tranquillity in their attack on religion.

Tocqueville never got over those books in the prefect's library in Metz, whose ideas shook his faith at the age of sixteen: "My life until then had flowed in an interior full of faith, which had not even allowed doubt to penetrate my soul." Afterward, doubt, universal doubt, poisoned his days. Roughly two years before his death he mentions the trauma of Metz again in a letter of February 26, 1857, to Madame Swetchine. A document of the first importance, the letter is both a confession and a cri de coeur. It begins on a slightly false note, with Tocqueville claiming that he "never found the slightest pleasure in examining myself closely." In fact, he was inveterately, endlessly introspective. In *Democracy in America*, for example, he wrote: "I need not traverse earth and sky to discover a wondrous object woven of contrasts, of infinite greatness and littleness, of intense gloom and amazing brightness, capable at once of exciting pity, admiration, terror, contempt. I have only to look at myself.... [Man] gropes forever, and forever in vain, to lay hold of some self-knowledge."

In this letter, he quickly changes course, confessing that he feels no uncertainty about his own weaknesses: "I believe my feelings and my desires are higher than my powers," he says, although part of his misfortune was to live at a time when ideals of the kind he cherished found no outlet in public life. He tells Madame Swetchine of his unseemly passion for success, "for being known, for renown which has animated me all my life; a passion which sometimes pushes one to great things, but which in itself is certainly not great." He thought he was cured of this problem after the success of *Democracy in America,* but worry about the reception of *The Old Regime and the Revolution* revived it. But then, he continues, "I have never been a completely reasonable man in any sense."

At a deeper level, he tells Madame Swetchine of his longing for certainty in a world that does not provide it. "The problem of human existence constantly preoccupies me and constantly overwhelms me. I can neither penetrate this mystery nor detach my eyes from it. In this world I find human existence inexplicable and in the other world frightening." He believes in another life, an afterlife, one in which people are rewarded and punished for their conduct on earth, but "everything beyond the bounds of this world seems to me surrounded by shadows which terrify me."

Tocqueville then alludes to the incident at Metz, which caused him to "be seized with the blackest depression, taken by an extreme disgust for life without having experienced it, and I was as if overwhelmed by trouble and terror at the road I had still to travel in the world." He is writing to Madame Swetchine now, near the end of that road, and, suffering repeated attacks on his fragile lungs, he must have known the end was very near.

The desolating news is that now, thirty-six years after Metz, he finds himself no less lost, possessed by the same feeling of devastation. "I see the intellectual world turn again and I remain lost and bewildered in this universal movement which overturns or shakes all the truths on which I have built my beliefs and actions. Here is a sad and frightening illness.... Happy those who have never known it, or who no longer know it." What was this illness? To believe in God, to feel even that one has glimmerings of understanding of God's complex reasoning, and yet not to be able to give oneself over to God—this would seem to be at the heart of Tocqueville's crisis, a crisis of faith. His inability to resolve this crisis left him in spiritual shambles.

Why Tocqueville should feel so bereft by the loss of religious faith may be difficult to understand in our own, more secular age, in which intellectuals and the putatively educated upper middle classes feel a certain pride in getting on so nicely without much thought about God. But we cannot dismiss the question as a mere historical curiosity.

Tocqueville's was of course a religious upbringing, and from all accounts a relatively happy one. Did he hope for a faith that would restore the confidence and stability he knew in those early years, when he felt certain of God's beneficence and all seemed right with the world? Tocqueville was too deep to settle easily or nonchalantly for atheism or agnosticism. To declare oneself an atheist, after all, is to agree to foreclose interest in the world's mysteries—in the origin and meaning of life, the point of the world's injustice and undeserved suffering, the possibility of an afterlife. To settle for agnosticism is to agree to forestall all such matters, holding them to be less than pressing, and to get on with the daily business of life. Neither atheism nor agnosticism seems a serious alternative for a brooding intelligence of the kind Tocqueville possessed.

Before his marriage, in 1833, Tocqueville wrote to his future wife: "I don't really know in truth what the range of my intelligence is, and I would be tempted to judge my intelligence very ordinary. But I believe I feel deep inside me, a soul more elevated than that of most men." When Tocqueville wrote the word "soul" he meant the sacred portion of one's being that comprises individuality, aspiration to do good, and generosity of spirit, all taken at the highest valuation, a valuation that is not self-conferred but divinely conferred.

Tocqueville's worries about the malaise of the soul under democracy no doubt derive from his regular, lifelong reading of Pascal. Pascal is mentioned or quoted four times in *Democracy in America*. Most significantly, Tocqueville brings in Pascal after writing of an "ardent, proud, and disinterested love of what is true." "Had Pascal," he writes, "had only some great profit in mind, or had he been moved solely by the desire for glory, I cannot believe that he would ever have been able to concentrate the powers of his mind as he did to uncover the Creator's best-kept secrets. Seeing him, as it were, wrest his soul in a way from life's concerns so as to devote [himself] entirely to his research, only to die of old age at forty, having prematurely ruptured the bond between soul and body, I stand amazed in the knowledge that no ordinary cause could have produced such extraordinary efforts."

Tocqueville admired Pascal too much not to take seriously what Pascal himself took most seriously of all: divination and proof of God's existence. "Being unable to cure death, wretchedness, and ignorance," Pascal wrote, "men have decided in order to be happy not to think about such things." Most men, perhaps, but not Alexis de Tocqueville. "Christianity," Pascal wrote, "is strange; it bids man to recognize that he is vile, and even abominable, and bids him to want to be like God. Without such a counterweight, his exaltation would make him horribly vain or his abasement horribly abject." Tocqueville needed only to look back on his own career to recognize this central truth. Ill, disappointed at the end of an active life, Tocqueville was perhaps more susceptible than ever before to Pascal's arguments, not least to that of his famous wager: "If you win [by believing in God] you win everything; if you lose you lose nothing."

One doesn't want to suggest that Tocqueville's last years were filled with religious torment. They weren't. His own moderation made that impossible: "I have always thought," he wrote to Louis Kergorlay, "that there was danger even in the best of passions when they become ardent and exclusive." At his remodeled estate in Normandy, he spent mornings working at his desk, afternoons in his fields at agricultural chores, evenings reading aloud with his wife before a large fire. In 1857, he took his last trip to England, where, feeling at home with the English aristocracy, he was everywhere feted as a great man. At the end of this trip, one of his English friends, Sir Charles Wood, arranged for a small ship, part of the British fleet, to return Tocqueville from Portsmouth to Cherbourg, and Tocqueville must have luxuriated in this Great Man treatment.

Tocqueville was never able to return to the second part of his book on the French Revolution, advancing, in rough draft chapters, only as far as 1787, two years before the actual revolution. Yet another lung attack—this one in 1857, not long after his return from England—brought on still further illnesses; and in 1858, he and wife repaired to the warmer climate of Cannes, where they rented a villa. There they were watched over by two nuns from the nearby Congrégation du Bon-Secours. It is far from clear when, exactly, Tocqueville began to sense that he was dying, though he began to invite, with some urgency, his dearest friends to visit him.

Alexis de Tocqueville died on April 16, 1859, not yet fifty-four. His death marked the final controversy of his career: whether or not he died a convinced Catholic. Gustave de Beaumont first claimed that Tocqueville did not require a deathbed conversion, because his faith had never truly lapsed; later he revised this claim to add that Tocqueville had many religious doubts. M. Jardin discovered a document in which Beaumont witnesses Tocqueville, shortly before his death, telling his wife, "Don't ever speak to me about confession—ever! Ever! No one will ever make me lie to myself and make a pretense of faith when I don't have faith. I want to remain myself and not stoop to telling lies!" This is reminiscent of George Santayana, spending his last years at the Hospital of the Blue Nuns in Rome, beseeching his protégé Daniel Cory that, no matter what the nuns might report, never to believe that he had undergone a deathbed return to the religion of his birth.

Beaumont goes on to report that his old friend, having been informed that a profession of faith in the dogmas of the Catholic church was not required for confession, did summon the curé of Cannes, to whom he made confession. Some say that Tocqueville did this to comfort his more devout wife. Others say that he slipped off and died a believing Christian, finding true solace at last in the sacraments of his church.

Kergorlay and Corcelle, the latter a serious Catholic, were both close friends of Tocqueville, and both visited him during his last days; but neither makes any mention of a return to the church. Later writers claimed that, as his literary executor, Beaumont, who had destroyed some of Tocqueville's letters and manuscripts and altered others, made up the story about his friend's state of incomplete belief—though nothing is known about Beaumont's having any antireligious feeling that might have impelled him to do so. M. Jardin, with his usual tact and good sense, suggests that, since it is impossible to know the condition of a man's soul, we shall never learn for certain whether Tocqueville, in the final days of his life, did or did not regain his faith.

This end to Tocqueville's life has a fit sense of ambiguity. Those with a religious cast of mind will hope that Tocqueville did indeed regain his faith; those able to live cheerfully without religion will prefer to believe that, like them, Tocqueville could depart life without resorting to the comfort of religion. Just as liberals find in Tocqueville a liberal, conservatives a conservative, aristocrats an aristocrat, and democrats a democrat, so now the religious and the unreligious can also have their own separate Tocquevilles. Alexis de Tocqueville, his body buried in the village of Tocqueville under a wooden cross, is certain not to object.

Epilogue

I N HIS THREE BOOKS, several notebooks, and hundreds of letters, Alexis de Tocqueville left a rich but scattered deposit of political wisdom. What he wrote does not constitute a system, or even a body of detachable or easily acquired ideas. Isaiah Berlin, who might be expected to have found Tocqueville's thought extremely attractive, wrote that he "was not a systematic theorist, nor a man given to (or even a connoisseur of) general ideas, nor a thinker of sufficient range and depth to cut across many fields of human thought and for that reason to be called philosophical." Berlin allows that Tocqueville "is an observer of genius, who clothed his aperçus in epigrams and aphorisms and sudden, arresting short-range generalizations; but he seldom, if ever, stirs thought with the force and boldness of a Hobbes or a Hume, or a Rousseau; he has not the systematic brain or moving directness of Mill; still less does he open windows on literally unfathomable depths like Hegel and Marx." Berlin's final verdict, damnation with faint praise, is this: "Tocqueville is highly original without seeking to build a system, and without ever raising his voice."

Is that, in the words of another nonsystematic thinker, Peggy Lee, all there is? After lingering over Tocqueville's writing for more than a year, I think there is a great deal more to be said on his behalf. Systematic thought must be a comfort to those who have the gift and taste for it, but of political systems one should have thought the world (for now, at least) has had quite its fill. "Human institutions can be changed," Tocqueville wrote, again evoking the influence of Pascal on his thinking, "but man cannot."

In France, the great writers recapitulate and extend their great precursors. So in reading Proust one thinks always of Stendhal and Balzac, and of how Proust absorbed them and then, in his intense psychological acuity, went beyond them. In Tocqueville's case, his precursors are Montesquieu (1689–1755) and Rousseau (1712–1778). Tocqueville took from Montesquieu his love of liberty; the notion that all the interrelated circumstances, historical and physical, of a nation's physiognomy must be studied; and much else—but rejected his notion that forms of government engender modes of behavior (monarchy, honor; aristocracy, moderation; republicanism, virtue; despotism, terror). Tocqueville showed that things often work the other way around, with modes of behavior just as likely to engender forms of government, and with mixtures often possible—a democratic monarchy, for example. From Rousseau Tocqueville took the notion that the age of aristocracy was finished, and the age of democracy irresistible. But he was less concerned with utopian justice and other political abstractions implicit in *The Social Contract* and in such thin conceptions of Rousseau's as the Noble Savage. As Proust with his precursors, so Tocqueville with his: he extended both Montesquieu and Rousseau through his understanding of the importance of customs, values, and beliefs, and by his keener sense of the complex combinations and contradictions that are part of human nature and human societies.

George Wilson Pierson describes Tocqueville's mind as "essentially 'binocular,'" and it is true that Tocqueville appeared able to see more widely and deeply than others. He had the rare gift of being simultaneously passionate and disinterested, able to find good things in bad, bad things in good. "I reproach equality not for leading men into the pursuit of forbidden pleasures," he wrote, "but for absorbing them entirely in the search for permitted ones." Impossible though it is to imagine him engaged in trade, Tocqueville nonetheless recognized that trade was "the natural enemy of all violent passions. It loves moderation, delights in compromises, and is most careful to avoid anger, making men inclined to liberty but disinclined to revolution."

Most people, Toqueville thought, will either believe things without knowing why, or not know what it is they ought to believe. But a third possibility exists, another "type of conviction—the reflective, self-assured conviction that grows out of knowledge and emerges from the agitation of doubt itself—[and] it will never be granted to more than a very small number of men to achieve it as a reward for their efforts." Tocqueville was not yet thirty when he wrote that; by the time of his death at fifty-three, he had arrived among those—one shouldn't say happy, but highly perspicacious—few.

As an anatomist of democracy, Tocqueville remains unsurpassed. No one has yet gone beyond his portrayal of the weaknesses and strengths of democracy; no one has had a surer sense of what a democratic government is likely and unlikely to accomplish. He understood, as we put it today, the trade-off of what was gained and what was lost with the advent of equality in modern life; and it is doubtful if anyone since has understood it more deeply.

Tocqueville perceived early that democracy presented a stellar example of the saddest of all dilemmas, those in which two good things clash with little compromise or resolution possible. The two good things in democracy, of course, are equality and liberty. One would think it not too much to ask to have both full justice and complete liberty, but this is not so easily arranged. Laws are necessary for a carefully calibrated fairness; certain constraints will be required, because if everyone is cut loose to do his best, many will fall hopelessly out of the race. Historically, the two chief possibilities have been a gentle good society and a cruel great one. The middle possibility, a gentle society that is also truly great, has not yet shown up. Hoping against hope, many of us continue to wish that one day it will. Tocqueville knew it wasn't likely to come about soon.

But neither his sagacity in understanding the mechanics and consequences of democracy nor his penetrating insight into its central dilemma is sufficient to explain why he is the important writer he remains in our day, and is likely to remain.

In 1834, in the heat of composing the first part of *Democracy in America*, Tocqueville wrote a letter to Charles Stoffels setting out his thoughts about style and about what makes for longevity in literature. Like all good Frenchmen, he began with Buffon, lightly disputing Buffon's famous aphorism about style and the man being one and the same thing. A man and his style are not entirely separable, Tocqueville knew; but when one has allowed that, one hasn't said much. "Show me the books which have remained, having as their sole merit the ideas contained in them," Tocqueville wrote. Not many such books exist, he also knew, and few have been added since his time. He then goes on to say that "without possessing a style which satisfies [him] in the least," he has studied style with great attention and has concluded: "There is in the great French writers, whatever the period you find them in, a certain characteristic turn of thought, a certain way of seizing the attention of readers which is proper to each one of them. I believe that one is born with this individual stamp; or at least I confess that I see no means of acquiring it.... But there is a quality common to all great writers; it serves in a fashion as the foundation for their style; it's on this base that each one then lays his own color. This quality is, very simply, *good sense*."

Good sense—order in presentation, using words with the most scrupulous precision, balanced judgment—does of course partially constitute great style, but only partially. What Tocqueville left out was the qualities he himself, even as a young man, possessed to a very high power: moral seriousness, a passionate desire to grasp the truth, and impartiality or honest disinterest in the pursuit of truth.

The only twentieth-century writer in English who commanded this same tone of moral seriousness was George Orwell. Both he and Tocqueville had the courage to go against the intellectual grain of their times and describe the world as they saw it. Because both were on a moral mission, each was, forgivably, rather humorless. Yet, good as he was, George Orwell, missing the spiritual element, hadn't anywhere near the depth of Alexis de Tocqueville.

Tocqueville spoke of the "small share of fame" that his writing brought him, but he also disbelieved "that writings such as mine could have the least influence in such times as these." He was correct about the failure of his own writing's influence on the life of his own time. Nor can anyone say with any certainty what influence it has had on future generations, though it has always been read by the most serious minds of the day. (In this connection, Robert Nisbet, in his essay "Many Tocquevilles," has shown that every age finds its own Tocqueville; that is, it finds in *Democracy in America* what is most relevant to its own concerns.) What would have surprised Tocqueville, one suspects, is the persistence with which his writings have remained alive, part of the conversation on the great subject of the importance of politics in life.

Tocqueville's writings have remained alive because the man who wrote them succeeded in his struggle to see the world steadily and to see it whole, and to do so with the intellectual honesty in the search for truth that we have come to call objectivity. Although never easy, objectivity is less difficult for the dispassionate writer. But Tocqueville achieved his objectivity without forgoing his own profound passion: to steer the world clear of disaster, to help men and women live unencumbered by servitude and with the freedom to achieve their own best dreams. "Objectivity," said Schopenhauer, "is genius." Objectivity of the kind possessed by the often troubled but always sapient Alexis de Tocqueville is precisely what the German philosopher had in mind.

Acknowledgments

The Eminent Lives series quite sensibly dispenses with footnotes and elaborate bibliographies, but I would be remiss to the point of immorality if I did not acknowledge the extent to which this book has been made out of the books of the many superior writers who came before me to write about Alexis de Tocqueville. Among these writers, I am most heavily indebted to André Jardin, J. P. Mayer, George Wilson Pierson, Seymour Drescher, James T. Schleifer, Roger Boesche, and François Furet. In my text I most frequently quote from the following among their books:

Furet, François. *Revolutionary France, 1770–1880.* Translated by Antonia Nevill. New Haven, Conn.: Basil Blackwell, 1992.

Jardin, André. *Tocqueville: A Biography.* Translated by Lydia Davis with Robert Hemenway. New York: Farrar, Straus, Giroux, 1988.

Pierson, George Wilson. *Tocqueville in America*. Baltimore: Johns Hopkins University Press, 1996.

Schleifer, James T. *The Making of Tocqueville's Democracy in America*. 2nd edition. Indianapolis: Liberty Fund, 1999.

Tocqueville, Alexis de. *Selected Letters on Politics and Society*. Edited by Roger Boesche; translated by James Toupin and Roger Boesche. Berkeley: University of California Press, 1985.

Finally, I wish to thank Jessica Fjeld, a gracious, penetrating, and talented editor for improving my manuscript in ways too numerous to mention.